SITUATING OURSELVES
I
C
E
A
A
N
AND PRECARITY

Edited by Murmurae
(Paula Cobo-Guevara and
Manuela Zechner)
and JOAAP (Marc Herbst)

1
Conditions

2
Situatedness

3
Displacement

4
Tactics

Appendix

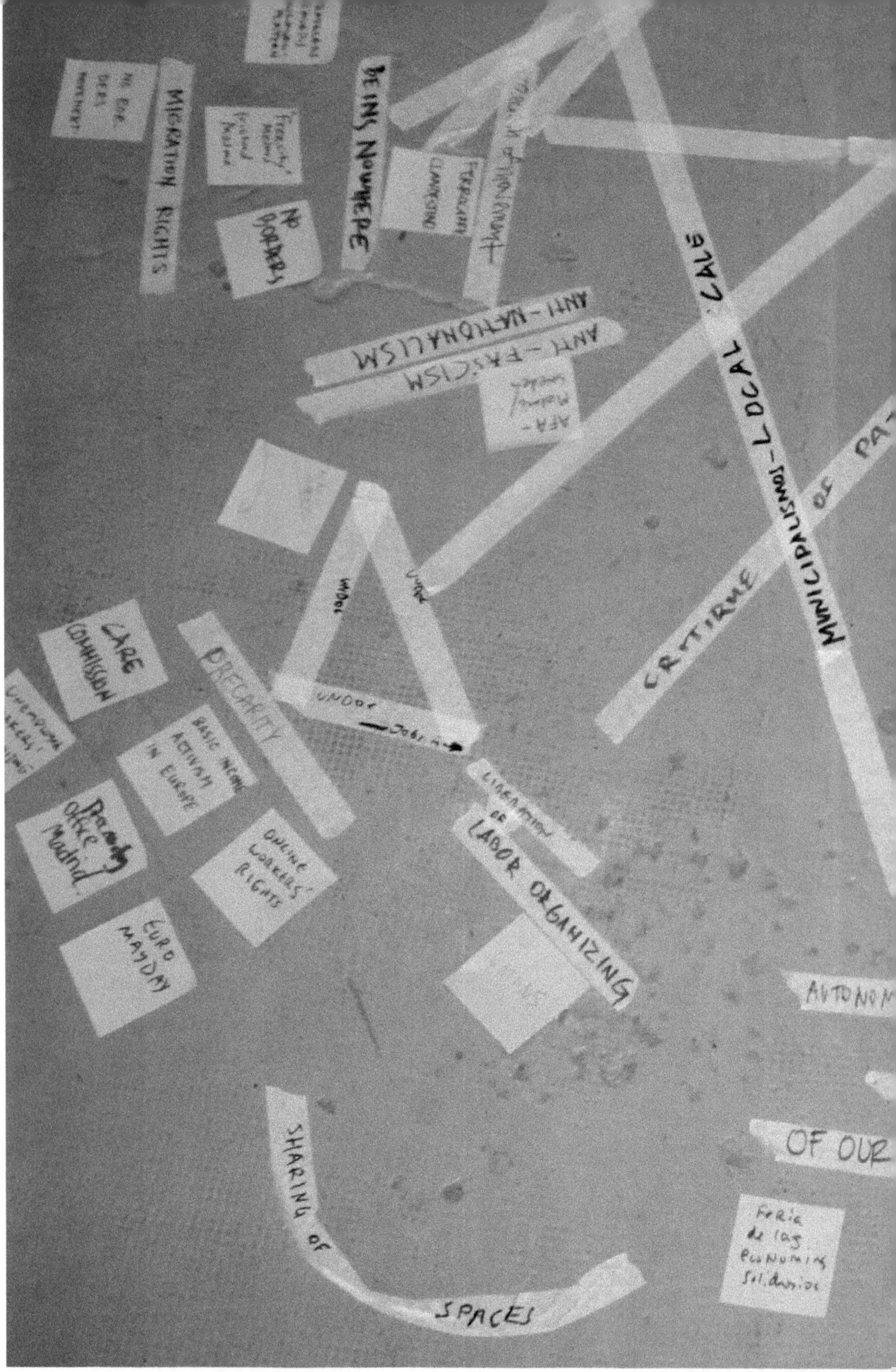

MIGRATION RIGHTS

BE INS NOWHERE

No Borders

CLEANSING

ANTI-FASCISM

ANTI-NATIONALISM

AFA-

MUNICIPALISMO - LOCAL CALS

CRITIRME OF PAT

CARE COMMISSION

PRECARITY

BASIC INCOME in Europe

ONLINE WORKERS' RIGHTS

EURO MAYDAY

Precarity Office Madrid

LABOR ORGANIZING

UMDS

AUTONOM

OF OUR

SHARING OF SPACES

Feria de las economias solidarias

What you have in your hands (or on your screen) is a collection-composition of texts that approach a problem we are trying to define – the relations between situatedness and displacement as embodied and subjective conditions. Our departure point for this is a collective gathering we organised in Autumn 2014, in Barcelona.

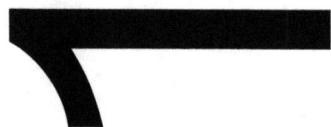

conditions

Situating ourselves collectively, and the problem of displacement: by way of an introduction.

by Manuela Zechner and Paula Cobo-Guevara

#neoliberalism   #positionality   #translation
#precarity   #composition   #micropolitics
#subjectivity   #mobility

DISPLACEMENT
AS A SHARED PROBLEM

When we launched the call for an autumn workshop in
2014, we departed from concerns that felt very intimate and
abstract at the same time. Displacement, as an embodied
verb, a felt fact, a new affect, was something we felt we shared
as condition – as condition of possibility as well as shared
impasse. We wanted to address the experiences, forms of
subjectivity, and material realities generated by displacement within neoliberal capitalism, starting from our own tra-
jetories. As transient subjects – caught between mobility
and migration, between precarity and flexibility – we noted that
displacement sometimes becomes a form of identity for
us. It constitutes a form of subjectivation (production of our
subjectivity) and subjectification (capture within a subjective paradigm) we feel ambivalent about, but know we cannot
escape. So we decided to explore this ambivalent reality
in a collective setting, to see if we can develop common analyses and find words to name our experiences, realities and
tactics – within, against and beyond displacement.

On the one hand, on a negative note, displacement relates
to the universes and universals of value of global capitalism,
to neoliberalism, to liberal subjectivity and cultural relativism,
to (neo)colonial (his)stories and to new and old modes of
exploitation. Becoming a migrant, a refugee, an undesired or
undocumented element; becoming a mobile subject, a
bundle of human capital, a self-entrepreneur of life, a creative
drifter. Histories of primitive accumulation, land grabbing
and being driven away. Universes of relativism and exchange
where any experience can stand in for any other, where we
are adrift in an abstract space, often captured by a liberalism
that converts any condition into a token. All these dynamics are characteristic of a logic of displacement that we think
is key to neoliberalism.

Exchange value, logistics, migration, human capital,
flexi-work, extractivism: we could draw a diagram of the lines

of force that run across these, and of how we each navigate within this field of contemporary power. Displacement implies all kinds of disempowering affects and existential dis-orientations: precarity, vulnerability, othering; unstable and contradictory relationships of belonging; loneliness, dis-orientation, anxiety[1]. These experiences of displacement reflect the reality of global capitalism, of bodies being intimately caught in value chains and logistical circuits.

Within this biopolitical configuration, displacement how-ever also has a positive meaning: it can mark a form of escape from those same forms of biopolitical control over our lives, a 'technology of self' that we appropriate in individual and also collective ways. We are also autonomous in our movements. Many knowledges spring from our experiences of moving – and with them many technologies, cultural forms, modes and platforms of relating that now shape our lives, from Facebook to Whatsapp, to Skype, etc – many knowledges and technologies respond to the global reality of displacement. Many attempts at hacking happen at this level. New transnational, translational and transductive sensi-tivities emerge from it, constituting new forms of agency and being political. The experience of living the elsewhere in multiple places and ways, of becoming other and outsider time and again, teaches us many a lesson about identity and subjectivity, and also about openness and solidarity. So we navigate a tension between cultural-economic liberalism and radical openings to (the) other(s).

INHABITING
DISPLACEMENT

What can we learn about the ways in which we inhabit this condition, when do we affirm and when do we resist dis-placement? If neoliberalism ceaselessly mobilises, how

1   Anxiety: when there are no clear reference points to hold on to, no markers to navigate by, when the stars blur into a shifting nightsky that we don't know how to read. Dizziness. Very different from fear, which always has a concrete object, which leaves us with a choice of fight/flight/faint. Anxiety escapes those tactics, it affects our whole being in the world from within. It acts on our vestibulary and reproduc-tive systems, amongst others, not just through the nervous or circulatory one. Anxiety and displacement go together.

and when and who do we mobilize? It makes a difference whether displacement comes disguised in a vast ocean of 'free' movements and precarious youthful mobilities, or comes slamming down as a form of control or discipline. The experiences, knowledges and tactics produced within these two polarities of displacement are different from one another. They produce specific forms of subjectivity that are often incompatible with each other, or pitted against one another: the migrant and the refugee, the precarious and the subaltern, etc. We situate ourselves in the attempts of thinking and acting across those. Of bridging the gaps that should keep us separate, of translating, situating, orienting, lending, hiding, trafficking, sharing, collectivizing.

13

The many stepping and stumbling stones via which displacement divides and rules – visas, permits, borders, non-rights, monolinguality, selective translation, short term contracts, conversion and cashing in – are also points of solidarity and struggle. Their techniques and technologies – encounters, chats, calls, marriages, money transfers, care networks – are deeply part of our everyday lives.

One of the functions of displacement is to make victims of us; another is to make heros. Beyond these two, and admitting a certain level of blurring and polyvocality between different experiences and conditions, we start from ourselves here, from an encounter in the Europe of the crisis. The idea here is to make the thin membranes between our existential, geographic and political territories touch and resonate. To think a micropolitics of displacement.

We are shaped by realities of dispersed friendships, families, relationships; scattered education and work trajectories; transitons between different movements, collective spaces; attempts at translating across different local histories… These conditions come with a series of effects. The skypification and whatsappification of relationships; the normalization of distance; frequent travel; applying for permits, jobs or grants in several continents at the same time; not quite knowing where to project ourselves; or when to know that we've 'landed'; the fragility and loneliness of being in a new place; the power of the networks that surround and hold us; the struggle to cultivate knowledges that come from different places; relearning how to inhabit relations of power and privilege; life-long language learning; etc.

SHARING
QUESTIONS

We came to these questions as newcomers in Barcelona, having just set up a feminist space in a small group – with the hope of establishing continuity and grounding ourselves collectively in a place and practice.[2] Therein we organised the autumn laboratory, which in turn attracted many new-comers, returners or escapees from other places. The texts you find in this publication are records, testimonies, echos and mirrors of the problems we addressed in this labora-tory, written by participants and workshop facilitators. We de-parted from questions which many texts here respond to:

↘What do politics and ethics mean in the context of frequent displacements? → How do we understand and give account of our positionality and trajec-tory as itinerant subjects? ↗What tools do we have for

2   The 'Electrodoméstica' was a space we collectively rented in Barcelona in 2014, aiming to set up a feminist cooperative to matching our lives and labours in new ways. A space for reproducing our lives in close connection with our communities, politics and material needs. This corresponded to a generational moment of exhaustion: having gone past 30 and still being on the move, unsure, without secure income. Our attempt failed. Not least because we each inhabited the space with different notions and stakes concern-ing 'reproduction': a tough lesson that taught us that it's not just reproduction that matters, as a radical buzzword that attracts us amidst a profound sense of unsustainable forms of life, but that the deeper political question is 'reproduce what'?

orienting ourselves in new contexts, for mapping out stakes,
problems and possibilities of relating?　↖ What does is mean
to struggle against precarity,
globalization and neoliberalism
in embodied terms?　↙ How
do we forge networks of care,
post-national struggles and
solidarities in our everyday?
　↓ How do we think consistency and sustainability?
　↗ What terms serve us to
think an ethics and politics of
displacement – situated/adrift,
local/global, intimate/alien-
ated, individual/collective, inde-
pendent/interdependent,
coming/going, flight/promise,
transversality/intersectionality?

displacement

migration mobility Flexibility

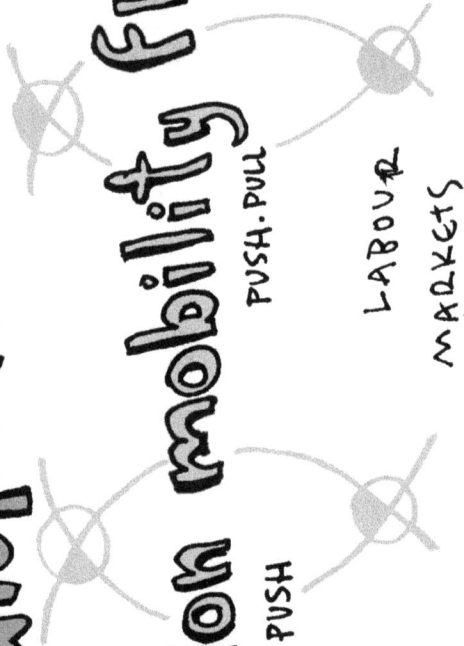

PUSH

PUSH·PULL

PULL

LAND

LABOUR MARKETS

PRECARITY

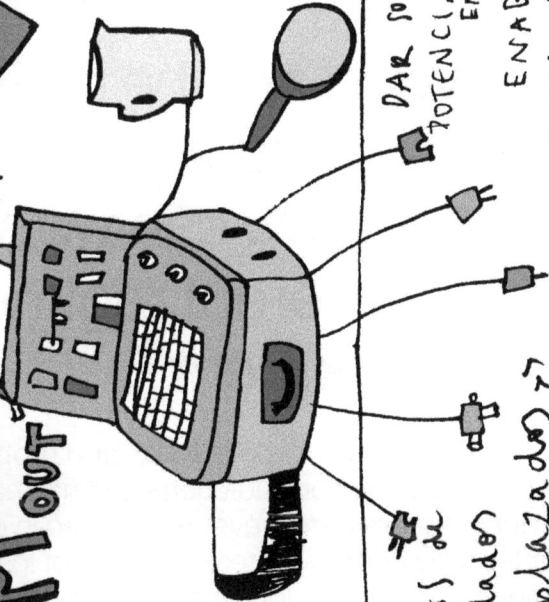

<< LOS MAPAS SE MUEVEN CON NOSOTRAS >>

CUIDADOS

mapping OUT

SI SE PUEDE

CARE MAP

1. looking after body of someone
2. Sharing resources
3. emotional attention
4. keeping the relation going

matices lenguas

LOOK AFTER — ACTITUDE
CUIDADOS — PRESTAR ATENCIÓN
PREOCUPARSE
語言?

5. Sharing experience + Knowledge
6. potentialism / enabling
7. setting limits

ESCUCHA / ATENCIÓN emocional
COMPARTIR RECURSOS
CUIDAR LOS CUERPOS
MANTENIMIENTOS
COMPARTIR CONOCIMIENTOS Y EXPERIENCIAS

DAR SOPORTE
POTENCIALIZAR EN COMÚN
ENABLE
PONER LÍMITES

<< MAPAS de cuidados desplazados >>

17

↓ When do we resist displacement and how do we resist through displacement? → What are the ways in which contemporary practices of displacement are produced by the neoliberal paradigm and embedded within structures and systems of governance? ↘What are the relations between mobility and migration? ↓ How can we struggle across different regimes of displacement?

We often inhabit uprootedness and mobility in very naturalised modes. The contradictions and normalisations of displacement are hardly ever addressed in collective ways: because they come with fear and guilt of losing the other, of infidelity, instability, loneliness, betrayal, abandoning a collective process or space. So displacement tends to be addressed in individualised, victimizing or psychologizing ways. His or her choice, his or her privilege, his or her misery, his or her problem. How many relationships and collectives have we seen suffer from and yet not deal with the fact that people are itinerant or leave? How few tools do we have to talk about the material, social and cultural forms of power that displacement mobilizes? What do we do with the loneliness, guilt, loss of vitality or confusion that come with the instability of displacement, and with the forms of social and cultural capital, non-commitment and relativism related to being on the move?

We mostly inhabit the paradoxes of transnational life without resolving them: or let's say, we resolve them in singular and particular ways that are never complete or universal. This booklet – following on from our laboratory – explores tactics and strategies through which we resolve the contradictions of displacement, testing if they can be collectivised and politicizes. One key desiring question for us is: what can it mean to 'settle' across more than one position or place, having gathered a baggage of translocal knowledges and relationships that commits us to two or more referents? Is there such a thing as an 'open relationship' with place/space? What can it mean to be 'faithful' or 'complicit' in collective processes across places and contexts?

The knowledges and forms of resistances we build in experiences of displacement are hard to speak about – because they're traversed by power as well as emotion – and yet they are crucial to our realities. We choose to call the resistant side of these knowledges and practices situatedness.

This project has served us for situating some of our experiences in our bodies and in social and historical context. We see how economic bubbles, exchange programmes, the Schengen and similar agreements, the cultural-creative industries and peak oil shaped our forms of life and subjectivity. We see how waves of (primitive or not) accumulation – of present and past crises – have shaped movement and care networks beyond the geopolitical and economic 'centre'. Somewhere, sometimes, often in uncharted territories, even in one and the same body, these different conditions and experiences meet. Or indeed across bodies. Many texts here speak to these encounters and crossovers of regimes of displacement.

Our interest is tactics and experiences that may open new political-compositional horizons. We want to create knowledges and practices that liberate – beyond the freedom of 'whatever' or the freedom of critique, beyond the usual liberal or enlightenment expressions of a universal subject. An embodied critique – there is too much consciousness and too many illuminated people around – that can help us subvert our own lives, 'so that the world cannot be the same any longer'[3]. Neither free to choose and be whatever – je ne suis pas Charlie – nor free to reject and dissociate ourselves from whatever – ich sehe das aber kritisch – : beyond the world wide web of disembodied speech and the blackmail of identity, with a politics of being somewhere, arriving somewhere, situating ourselves in relation to others and together with others. The somewhere of nowhere, and the nowhere of somewhere, also the now.here need to be taken into account for that.

One problem with displacement is the (neo)liberal subject that puts itself easily into the place of any other, speaks in the name of any other, assumes and subsumes any 'knowledge' in its machine of equivalences, doesn't recognize that difference can cut deep and that not everything can be said from everywhere equally. Which ignores that subjectivity is largely about articulations with power, meaning that where you can speak from, how you relate and what you embody is to do with power. Subjectivity is about power even when it is about care and gestures of commoning – rather than being about a happy-go-lucky puzzle game of constituting one's identity or lifestyle (as many anglo-saxon readings of Foucault, Deleuze and Guattari have it).

That same subject position often affirms art as a universal language of technique and ideals within which any gesture goes, any statement is fine, any speculation valid. Or that

3   Marina Garcés, <u>Encarnar la Crítica</u>, Espai en Blanc – our translation, our emphasis.

'freedom of speech' matters more than situated, embodied, listening and respectful ways of speaking. That there is such a thing as a right to be universal, that freedom is about affirming this privileged position. We're interested in crystallizations that generate new self-positionings, new references, forms of enunciation beyond this; in processes that enable action, praxis. There's no such thing as a subjectivation that's adrift – there are adrift subjectitivities alright, but no such thing as a process of whatever subjectivation.

So part of the answer to the question of overcoming the liberal condundrum has to do with situated embodiments of knowledges. Akin to the situated knowledges Donna Haraway speaks of in her critique of the scientific paradigm[4] of partial knowledge, we want to critique the liberal paradigm of total knowledge and its cyber(dis)embodiments. This is not about rejecting technoscience, technopolitics or research, but about developing radical and situated practices in sustainable ways. Radical meaning not so much unshakably ooted as solidly grounded perhaps. Grounded in collective subjects and in embodied ways of knowing and inhabiting.

How do we construct a collective narrative that breaks away from the hyper-individualized narratives of displacement that we see on our screens and in our communities – from the spectacle of displacement as migration or mobility? This project has been a space for us to experiment with situated and intimate articulations beyond the immediate spectacle of social media, to which so much of our time goes these days. The texts in this publication explore narratives and articulations in the first person, singular and plural. Yet we have flirted with social media. We leave you some profile pictures from friends in our social networks.

4   Haraway, Donna (1988) Situated Knowledges: The Science Question in Feminism and the Privilege of Partial Perspective. In: Feminist Studies, Vol. 14, No. 3. (Autumn, 1988), pp. 575–599.

conditions

(por que Ithaca hedía a zapatilla nike)

cabalgando sobre el lomo de la yegua
caminante del camino

¿a qué jugaban los hijos de los exiliados?

Ah nosotros jugábamos a tirarles piedra a los pacos,jajajaja saludos

os amo os adoro! sois lo máximo!

Some motions and meditations on displacement

by Laura Lapinskiene

#displacement   #migration   #common(s)
#neoliberalism   #place   #micropolitics
#precarity

In the middle of a collective jam session in an underground punk club "Kablys" in Vilnius in 2011, G. stops playing his sax, picks up a microphone and screams in Lithuanian: Lietuva jau laisva, galit daryt ka norit su ja! ("Lithuania is already free – you can do whatever you want with her!"). This pronouncement blends in with the noise of drums, guitar, synths in a stream of consciousness, and rather poignantly expresses the feeling of the moment: these are the times when you are "free" to choose your identity and your lifestyle according to confrontational, "alternative" culture, like punk, metal or vegan, or just be a good citizen-consumer-subject, whatever! However, the structural processes of dispossession and displacement are going on without much public contestation, while corrupt local elites can do whatever they want – since "Lithuania is already free!" Free Lithuania was one of the most publicly pronounced slogans during the "singing revolution" of the 1990s. G. recalls that he and many of his artist friends participated in these contentious events, highly anticipating the promised change. However, over subsequent years of freedom he, like many others, was deeply disenchanted.

With political independence, came confusion, obscurity, uncertainty and non-functionality (Balockaite 2008).[1] The only thing to replace dead communism were capitalism and democracy achieved by means of voluntary westernization. The economic development of Lithuania since the restoration of independence in 1990 has not been linear. Immediately after 1990 there was a rapid decline in the economy, following the restructuring of industry, the initiation of land reforms and the privatization of state companies. Such shifts kicked off a wave of migration with many people dispersing around the globe in search for better conditions. After Lithuania joined the EU in 2004, the processes of emigration greatly accelerated: in the period between 1990

25

1   http://www.eurozine.com/articles/
2008-05-08-balockaite-en.html

and 2006 nearly half a million citizens left the country[2]. In 2010, he number of emigrants reached unprecedented heights: 38 500 people left in 2009 and in 2010 this number doubled (83 157)[3], leaving less than 3 million remaining in Lithuania. So 2.97 out of a total 3.6 million Lithuanians live scattered around the globe[4].

Citizens of this place have increasingly voted with their feet and left to work in the prosperous Western countries, instead of voicing their concerns to local or national politicians. Their disillusionment was augmented by the high expectations of a better life that struggles for independence had promised to realize. What does it mean for Lithuania and its people? From the perspective of political rhetoric, such migration tendencies pose great challenges in terms of ageing of the population, anticipated labour and skills shortages, brain drain and imaginary danger of a disappearing nation. This discourse reinforces dichotomies by accusing people who leave (betrayal) and instilling a sense of pride in those who stay (commitment). On both political and individual levels, there is a lot of resentment coupled with patriotism – only a stone's throw from turning into nationalism – when it comes to Lithuania's outmigration. But on the other hand, there are powerful networks of informal social support and the sense of waiting for returnees with the new skills, better attitudes and fresh enthusiasm. Migration opens an ambivalent field of feelings, discourses and be/longings, marking the very private as well as public spheres.

As a consequence of mass migration, the public sphere was found to be shrinking: the absence of visible public participation has been often referred to as a "non-existing civil society" in Lithuania. Whether such claims only reproduce the myth of passive masses[5], which is created and sustained through hegemonic discourses and daily practices, remain the point of inquiry. However, it is clear that the ones who stay

2   http://osp.stat.gov.lt/services-portlet/pub-edition-file?id=3032
3   The Department of Statistics (2014).
4   The Department of Statistics (2014);
http://db1.stat.gov.lt/statbank/SelectVarVal/
saveselections.asp (2014).
5   See article by Noah Brehmer Lithuania: Myth of the passive
masses (https://libcom.org/library/myth-passive-masses).

within the national borders for extended periods of time are trying hard to make sense of everyday realities, deal with the broken promises, precarity and even poverty, cope with individualized misery, challenge lack of collective attempts and political will.

Sometimes it is pretty hard to determine who is staying and who is leaving. Some of those who were determined to "stick to the place" are now some thousands kilometers away from Europe. Many of us are just moving around, living "in between" places, being everywhere, or rather nowhere. In current neoliberal terms, we have become "mobile experts", "freelancers", "world citizens", "global nomads" who might in certain cases translate into "precariat", "non-belonging", "forced migration", "dispossession", and most certainly – "displacement".

The following photo-dialogues seek to illustrate people's attempts to articulate and make sense of their precarious situations and ambiguous states of being, trajectories perceived as choices, decisions or spontaneous moves, confrontations and critiques expressed through music, art and movement, in every sense of the word.

L HOW DO YOU FEEL?

G How do I feel!? I feel the way I look. I try 'to be' as much as I can. What else is there left for me – 'not to be'? I want 'to be' if I already 'am'.[6] However, many things keep bothering me. I have no money to pay for gas, electricity. Small problems. That's why I'm playing, beating my drum – in order not to think about these problems.

L AND HOW DO YOU LIKE LIVING IN KAUNAS?

G F*** Kaunas! I really hate it here! This city is ruled by thieves! And it's full of chamas[7], too. I'm desperate to get out of here!

L WHERE WOULD YOU LIKE TO GO?

G I don't care, to the forest, to nature, to the cosmos, whatever! Really, this is not the question – where. Of course, I want to go there and there; now I even got a new permit to

6   In 2012, the leading country for suicide was Lithuania, with a suicide rate of 34.1 per 100,000 inhabitants. It is particularly high for men around 40 – 50 years of age. It can be a struggle to hold on to life. (http://www.ncbi.nlm.nih.gov/pmc/articles/PMC3367275/).
7   Chamas is a common "nickname" in Lithuania, apparently derived from a word chamstwo used in Poland to describe rude behavior in public space. These small violent ways people relate to each other in urban public space become part of the daily routine and go largely unnoticed. However, it becomes striking after living abroad for a while or starting to reflect on your personal daily encounters. As Kacper Poblocki (2010) nicely puts it, "not direct violence, but all the small things that make the urban experience enervating, stressful and unpleasant." (see Poblocki, K. (2010). The Cunning of Class: Urbanization of Inequality in Post-War Poland, PhD dissertation; pp. xii).

conditions

go to America and have a place to stay there, but my current concern is to solve those financial problems.

G   Sure, there was change with 'freedom of movement' and 'freedom of expression', but it mostly brought 'freedom to grab whatever you can' during the transition to the free market economy. I think it is even worse now for the artists and majority of people in Lithuania than it was during Soviet times. In those times, you at least had a common enemy – an alien government – something to fight against. Now, everyone is interested only in his/her own thing. You cannot point the finger at anything – where the hell is the enemy really? You feel dispossessed and out of place, but whom to blame?

A   When I hitchhike in Lithuania and people ask me where am I from, I tell them I am from Lithuania. But of course, then I have to explain myself. I have to tell them that I am born in one place, live in another, study, work, spend holidays and do shopping in yet other places. Each activity takes place in a different city; I live my life on a Lithuanian scale.

A   Now I am departing to another country. I do it because I have to.

L   WHY DO YOU HAVE TO?

A Because of my Karma.

L   DO YOU FEEL DISPLACED?

A Sometimes I feel so out of place! I want to live on the land, in the countryside, away from the city. And yet, I am imprisoned in these urbanities – between the walls, physical and imagined. […] You know, I wanted to make a hole in the wall in order to connect two rooms, so I took a big hammer and did it. I think I will hammer my way out of here…

J After the last high-school exam I left the classroom, went to the yard and asked for a cigarette to contemplate the occasion. My whole body could feel the change of balance towards something very heavy. I can recall the moment I recognized this and started thinking: I've grown tired of doing a constant countdown. When will it suffice to suffer? Two months until the Christmas holidays. Three days until the weekend. Two classes until I can go home. Twelve minutes until the break. Three years before I take my exams… I am tired of this countdown. What happens if time starts to pass in a natural course without counting it down? I could feel an infinite excitement.

conditions

J I realize that I have the best knowledge of social space as it is in Lithuania. However, now I feel that it does not necessarily benefit me. The form of existence and communication that is there is not satisfactory. I start getting a certain feeling of loneliness, while my connection to this place gradually weakens.

J Many people are leaving; or at least moving all the time. It is easy to lose connection when you are not present. I mean, being constantly on the move distances you from places and people. Sometimes it's like a vicious circle: I am distanced from here due to movement, but the more I am distanced, the easier it gets to move, to go somewhere again. And naturally I start asking myself, 'What the hell am I doing here?'

L   WHAT MAKES YOU MOVE?

R   I would not say that I move much. I think I am the kind of person who doesn't like/ need too much mobility. I just changed few places (countries) over the past 10 years, that's all. You know the saying 'the grass is greener on the other side', and for me it is the oppo- site – I think that I need to find the way to live in the place where I am at the moment. I can't say I necessarily love the place I live in, but I need to handle it the best I can.

L   SO DO YOU FEEL THAT YOU FOUND YOUR PLACE?

R   No, absolutely not. I don't think there is such thing as 'my place'. I think I consciously chose a path, which does not require or even allow for having or finding one's place.

L   DO YOU FEEL IN ANY WAY DISPLACED, THEN?

R   I wouldn't say that either. I feel that I have never been 'placed', I never had my place as such, and so I can't really feel the displacement.

R   Sometimes, it is even hard for me to imag- ine that a place could be interesting. It happens that if I go to some place else, I always meet the same kind of people, and have the same kind of conversations, which brings me back to the same conclusion that it is not the place that really matters.

L WHY DO YOU KEEP MOVING?

S   I haven't found my place yet and, maybe, I don't want to find it. You stay in one place for a while, and then you want to move and stay in another. We have countless possibilities and I want to use them. In order to settle down in one place, there must be something to bind one to a certain place in terms of geographical location, isn't it? And it's not the things or people that does that, but rather the state of mind. And so it happens that I am not bound to a certain place. I have no land. Besides, the world is big and I want to see it.

L DO YOU FEEL DISPLACED?

S   Sometimes I do, sometimes I don't, like everyone else, no? There are times when I don't want to go anywhere or to do anything. But at other times, for example, I want to do things. Now I want to travel. And sometimes you can feel very lonely while travelling. But you meet people when you are away from home.

S   Home is the place to which you can return, lie down on your bed and sleep tight. Where there is a bed and it is not cold. Not necessarily, but it's good if it's not cold. Well, yeah, it's basically a pleasant place to return to. Home… Perhaps, your friends live there. And dogs… In fact, 'home' used to designate a place, when I was a child and had my home where I grew up. But now it's more about people, about the ones I feel attached to. Anyhow, even at home you feel good and bad…

L   WHY DO YOU KEEP MOVING?

U   When I see examples of people who are close to me, and observe the lives of my family – my mom, dad, grandparents – I realize I don't want such a destiny that is bound to constant, sedentary existence, which at the end becomes total seclusion and there is no more contact. In my opinion, there is no more meaning to such life. Perhaps that's what makes me move, travel, search, meet people. But I cannot say that there's only one major reason why I keep moving. It's a search for knowledge, love, passion, money and the lack of all those things.

L   HOW DO YOU DEFINE YOUR PLACE?
DO YOU FEEL DISPLACED IN ANY SENSE?

U   For me, there is no 'my place', because there are many places that I feel connected with. What connects me is the people who stay in those places and memories that I carry in my head. As well as future plans. Although I would very much love to say that my place is simply the place where I am

conditions

at the moment – but I guess I can't say that 100 percent. It's not that I travel to any corner of the planet and feel comfortable and secure, I always need some time to feel attached to a place. I think my places are the ones that no longer require time to feel attached to. So yes, I feel displaced, but I like it to a certain extent. It gives me more ways to look at the places that I'm connected to. Sometimes I feel displacement just because I can't afford the plane tickets back to Lithuania, for example. It's too far, and the tickets are too expensive. Sometimes I have no time to come back. Sometimes I wish I could have time, and then I feel that friction and displacement.

L   WHAT MAKES YOU MOVE?

O   What makes me move? Normally, the call of the heart, and even if I'm already 'moved' all the places that I have seen, all the roads I have travelled still come up in my mind as day dreams. So sometimes I have a week where I walk down the streets here in Guatemala but my heart is on an Estonian island or on the ocean shores, or in Portugal… Then, I remind myself that I am in such an amazing place and that one day, I will be daydreaming of Antigua's central park and the volcanoes…

L   DO YOU FEEL DISPLACED?

°   I do feel displaced. This was, probably, why I kept on going… and going… no matter where I went. I feel good in Lithuania, but something inside me feels like I don't have a place there. Once I came to live in Guatemala I had that same feeling and what I did was that I said to myself 'you have the right to live here just like anyone else. You have the right to walk and you have the right to have your favourite bookstore'. Now I feel better and I feel that I can 'occupy the space'. But still! I want to travel and see other places, and live in them, and discover other book-stores and other shores of the same ocean… (It is always about the shore…)

conditions

L   WHAT MAKES YOU MOVE?

A   Interesting things, people, landscapes... The fact that I am a curious duck helps me move away from Kaunas. And also the fact that even though I could maintain a stable monthly income here to buy potato chips, elsewhere it seems easier. But at the end of the day, all roads lead to Kaunas, so we will meet there, you will see!

37

L   DO YOU FEEL DISPLACED?

A   I don't really feel displaced in terms of geographical location. However, I feel displaced from the futurities that might have happened. Not so much from the concrete places and times, but more from the zones of intensities and magic.

Colonial and Cannibal Orientations

by Bue Rübner Hansen

ROBINSON CRUSOE
AS GUIDE AND MYTH

Cyclones, capital investments, career opportunities. War, drought, and floods: the nomadic and the sedentary are increasingly swept along or overflowed by translocal and global forces. How to orientate oneself when you are adrift in a tempest or when the ground below you shakes in an earthquake? Such processes lead to a problem of orientation. How to orientate oneself in displacement, when one is not a part of a stable cosmos, social order or life world? While we cannot presume that this problem was inaugurated by European modernity (as if "pre-modern" people somehow lived homeostatic, circular, organic lives), it is true that European modernity – with its colonisation and capitalist globalisation – has continually posed the problem of orientation with urgency, overflowing and uprooting people across the globe.

To understand the emergence of the problematic of orientation in modern western philosophy, one must turn to narratives of geographical disorientation in the meeting between modern capitalist Europe and its others. Here, at the beginning of the bourgeois epoch, we sense that orientation is always more than geographical. The aim of this text is to clarify the modern problem of orientation through a reading of one of the great modern myths of western man, namely Daniel Defoe's novel Robinson Crusoe (1719). Looking back, this novel can be read as a modern myth describing the historical construction of the individualised, male, western subject, which became the hegemonic form of orientation in capitalist modernity. The book, however, did not only express this orientation, it contributed to it. Translated in more than a hundred languages, published in innumerable editions, and inspiring a great number of narratives, the book's influence is indisputable. And its influence is more profound than its spread, for books are often read and forgotten by millions, while Robinson was a pedagogical orientational manual for the readers, a veritable dispositive of subjectivation.

Robinson Crusoe expressed and participated in the creation of the still hegemonic form of orientation within the modern problem of displacement, and it entails a certain articulation of need and desire, a certain relation to the other and to nature. The deconstruction of this model of masculine individualism, which this text seeks to contribute to, opens for a consideration of other orientational responses to the displacements of capitalist modernity.

Through an investigation of the disorientation and reorientation of the Robinson myth, the aim of this text is to provide a materialist and existential concept of orientation that avoids the usual understanding of Robinson as the literary exposition of human nature, or as purely ideological figure. Discussing the conditions of the strength of the Oedipus myth, Deleuze and Guattari quoted Jacques Lacan's precise statement, which goes against any Jungian idea of invariable Ur-myths: "a myth cannot sustain itself when it sustains no ritual".[1] This attunes us to how the effectivity of the Robinsonian myth, in turn, relies on the rituals it supports. This is an insight that will be extended in two directions. Firstly, if the effectivity of myths is materially grounded in rituals, rituals in turn rely on broader social pragmatics, composed of needing and desiring bodies. The question then, is not merely what the meaning of myth is, but what role a myth plays in sustaining certain pragmatics. Secondly, no matter how fantastical and removed its narrative content is rom the everyday social pragmatics, myth must share a common form with social practice in order to sustain it. The myth must orientatable, to be source of orientation. What matters is not the concept of myth as a map, but that it shares cartographic coordinates with social practice. Thus the study of Robinson Crusoe will help us understand the existential and practical stakes that continue to give life to the Robinsonian man, who Derrida humorously called Homo Robinsoniensis.[2] Many readings of Robinson Crusoe remain satisfied with deconstructing Robinson's anthropocentrism,

1   Lacan in Gilles Deleuze and Felix Guattari
Anti-Oedipus: Capitalism and Schizophrenia, New Ed
(London: Continuum, 2004), 83.
2   Jacques Derrida, The Beast and the Sovereign
(University of Chicago Press, 2011), 198.

colonialism, possessive individualism or masculinity; in this text, the focus on Robinson as a dispositive of orientation will enable us to raise the question of other possible orientations in relation to displacement, alternatives to being or becoming Robinson.

ROBINSON CRUSOE,
THE TEACHER

41

The cultural and historical meaning of the Robinson Crusoe narrative is well established, and it must be understood in its profound ambivalence. In 1857 Marx noted that this novel was written in "anticipation of 'civil society', in preparation since the sixteenth century and making giant strides towards maturity in the eighteenth" (1857 Introduction). Similarly, in a lecture at the Popular University of Trieste in 1912, James Joyce also describes Robinson Crusoe as a literary prefiguration:

> The whole Anglo-Saxon spirit is in Crusoe: the manly independence; the unconscious cruelty; the persistence; the slow yet efficient intelligence, the sexual apathy, the practical, well-balanced religiousness; the calculating taciturnity. Whoever rereads this simple, moving book in the light of subsequent history cannot help but fall under its prophetic spell.[3]

In his seminal study of individualism in early modern literature, Ian Watts notes that while the individualist figures of renaissance novels such as Don Quijote or Don Juan were ridiculed and punished for their individualism, Defoe celebrates and rationalises Robinson's.[4] Just as Joyce's and Marx's commentary this suggests that Robinson Crusoe bears witness to the emergence of what Raymond Williams has called a change in the structure of feeling. It is, following Williams, a text which expresses an emergent form

3   "Daniel Defoe" James Joyce, Occasional, Critical and Political Writing, ed. Kevin Barry and Conor Deane (Oxford University Press, 2000).
4   Ian Watt, Myths of Modern Individualism: Faust, Don Quixote, Don Juan, Robinson Crusoe (Cambridge University Press, 1997).

of life, whether it is prefigurative of, contemporary with, or an imminent successor to other widespread changes in the social formation.[5] Marx and Joyce show how the book's is an expression of its epoch, its protagonist a personification of the abstract social forces of capitalism and colonialism. The route, then, is short to show how Defoe's positive rendering of Robinson provides a literary apology for those forces. However, Robinson must be understood as more than a reflection or representation of something that exists. Like the distinction Marx draws between vulgar economists and political economists proper, Robinson Crusoe is not merely a vulgar and superficial apology, but an answer to lived problems. Thus, Defoe's novel is a meditation on the problem of the displacement of the modern subject. It is a narrative rendering of how a displaced subject can find its bearings through the submission of subjectivity, territory and others to its plan, a veritable catalogue of orientating techniques.

Like political economy, Defoe's discourse avoids both the crass empiricism and abstract romanticism that characterises vulgar economics and regular romance novels. They both construct logical fictions, a kind of speculative realism starting from simple atomistic premises such as the rational action of the isolated individual. Defoe carefully renders the otherwise exotic adventures of Robinson believable, and avoids any alienation of the reader through fantastic descriptions, while insisting that the story is "true". It is true, as is revealed in the third volume of Robinson Crusoe, not because it actually happened, but because it describes how an individual must act in order to survive in separation from others, i.e. as an individual. Defoe focusses on the practical challenges facing Robinson, rendering him trustworthy through the honesty of his confessional moments. The use of auto-biography invites the reader to identify with Robinson. The text does not present Robinson at a distance as a character to observe, instead the act of reading becomes the reproduction of Robinson's monologue in the form of the reader's inner voice. Further, Defoe goes through great effort

42

conditions

5   Raymond Williams, Structures of Feeling, in Marxism and Literature (Oxford: Oxford University Press, 1977).

to make the reader empathise with the practical and psychological problems Robinson faces, and the enjoyment of reading comes from the pleasure of seeing these prolems resolved through pragmatic ability or moral self-questioning. Robinson Crusoe not only reads as a guide to the conquest of unknown lands and subject populations, but as a guide to the conquest and improvement of the habits and soul. The broad appeal of the book does not lie so much in its apology for the powers of capitalist modernity, as much as in its realism and pragmatism, which build on Defoe's research into the oral histories of mariners and travellers to the new world.[6] It is often claimed that Defoe drew on the narrative of the cast-away Scottish mariner Alexander Selkirk who survived four years on a pacific island, but Defoe's research went deeper, and included interviews with seamen and, as Tim Severin has shown, a possible personal acquaintance with Henry Pitman, who had undergone events very similar to Robinson.[7]

The pedagogical character of Robinson Crusoe was already noted by Rousseau, who in his famous pedagogical tract Emile stated that the book was the only piece of literature necessary for the education of an autonomous, practical individual. To support this use, Rousseau suggested that the book should be cut down to the parts that deal with Robinson's years on the island[8] which would purify the conception of Robinson as a self-made man, who has to develop his own skills from scratch, and overcome the alienation of the social division of labour. Later, Marx noted that Robinson Crusoe is a narrative of unalienated labour: Having no boss, Robinson controls his own labour process and the products of his efforts.[9] Thus Defoe did not only eulogize colonial bourgeois subjectivity, he created a morality

6   Marcus Rediker, Outlaws of the Atlantic: Sailors, Pirates, and Motley Crews in the Age of Sail (Beacon Press, 2014), 34.
7   Tim Severin, In Search Of Robinson Crusoe (Basic Books, 2009), 328.
8   Thereby the narrative would have come closer to one of Defoe's inspiration's, the 12th Century tract حي بن يقظان (Philosophus Autodidactus) written by the Andalucian polymath Ibn Tufail, a narrative of a feral child which is raised by a gazelle on a desert island and discovers truth without human contact.
9   Karl Marx, Capital: Volume I, trans. Ben Fowkes (London: Penguin Books, 1976), 170.

tale about the value of hard work and the pleasure of its fruits, which was to resonate with exploited proletarians and landless peasants as well as bourgeois entrepreneurs and settler colonists (and tempt some of the former to strive to become the latter).

Thus, Robinson's fictional auto-biography provides a basic phenomenology of orientation within the capitalist epoch, starting from displacement. It deals with the practical challenges of satisfying bodily needs in new or changing environments, the development of new techniques of navigation and production, the separated individual who must desire to become productive to survive. It understands the cartography of orientation as a mapping of resources, possessions and territories, as a technology of appropriation and exclusion. This phenomenology of the castaway's orientation reveals a new political economy and geo-politics of orientation that has – to a large but contested extent – shaped the world in which we live, and the ways in which this reduces the other to trading partner, enemy or servant. As participants in that globalised 'civil society' we can call capitalist civilisation, we are all to some extent Robinson, and especially those of us who have been shaped or are shaping ourselves in the image of "Man" – white, independent, mobile. This is not necessarily because we believe in Robinson, identify with him, but certainly because Robinsonian techniques are forms of orientation that continually propose themselves as ways to deal with displacement.

A VERY MALE
REBELLION OF DESIRE

In Robinson Crusoe, the eponymous protagonist recounts the narrative of how he survived 28 years shipwrecked on a deserted island. From the beginning we learn that Robinson comes from a secure middle class family, his father a very "ancient", wise patriarch. While Robinson came from the mother's family, Crusoe was a corruption of his father's German name Kreutznaer. Kreutznaer advised the young Robinson to stay in his place and follow the middle path of life, which was the best state in the world, the most suited to human happiness, not exposed to the miseries and hardships, the labour and sufferings of the mechanic part of mankind, and not embarrassed with the pride, luxury, ambition, and envy of the upper part of mankind.[10]

Robinson is born into a profoundly content middle class, which is neither slave to need nor to desire.[11] But, as Minaz Jooma has pointed out, Robinson's guaranteed sustenance within his father's household is also a submission to patriarchal command. Kreutznaer goes as far as threatening Robinson with the withdrawal of subsistence if he disobeys him, like his brothers did.[12] Robinson soon tears himself out of the grasp of the family and the safe patriarchal place of guaranteed reproduction. Even if he does not consider this fact, he can tear himself away from the family because he is not caught up in its responsibilities the way that his mother is. Is it possible he only needs to tear himself away to seek freedom, because it is the father rather than the mother who dictates the terms of participation in familiar consumption? When speaking of leaving the family, Robinson continually uses the world desire, both when he speaks of the reasons for his brother leaving (which got him killed in war), and to describe his own motives to go to sea, which consists in pursuing "a rash and immoderate desire of rising faster than the nature of the thing admitted".[13] Robinson and Defoe

10   Daniel Defoe, The Life and Strange Surprizing Adventures of Robinson Crusoe, of York, Mariner: Who Lived Eight and Twenty Years All Alone in an Un-Inhabited Island on the Coast of America, Near the Mouth of the Great River of Oroonoque; Having Been Cast on Shore by Shipwreck, Wherein All the Men Perished But Himself: With an Account How He Was at Last as Strangely Deliver'd by Pyrates. Written by Himself (W. Taylor, 1719), 3, henceforth "RC".
11   During this period, middle class referred to the class below the nobility and above the common people. Thus middle class referred to the bourgeoisie and petty bourgeoisie. What is interesting in our context is not the economic definition of this class and the transformations of the semantics of "middle class", but to study the subjective orientation of Robinson's middle class, through which we can create a genealogy of subjectivity today. "Middle Class" in Raymond Williams, Keywords: A Vocabulary of Culture and Society (Routledge, 2011).
12   Jooma in Kristen Guest, Eating Their Words: Cannibalism and the Boundaries of Cultural Identity (SUNY Press, 2014).
13   Defoe, The Life and Strange Surprizing Adventures of Robinson Crusoe, of York, Mariner, 43.

clearly understand desire as a force of displacement, an orientation that pushes the subject beyond inhabitation,
beyond sedentary forms of life. But this desire is already a
male, patriarchal desire. He does not merely seek the
freedom o sustain himself or sustain himself with others, but
to "rise", that is to gather the resources to create a household of his own with the dependants that this entails.

In its implicit philosophy of desire and need, the text shows
how closely the opposition between freedom and necessity correlates not only with the patriarchal logic of the oikos,
but also with the anthropological machine that produces
the difference between animals and human beings. That his
father's warning speaks of the lower parts of mankind
as "mechanic" is not insignificant, but a reminder of René
Descartes' theorisation of animal being as purely me-
chanical. By birth Robinson is elevated above the animal concern to find water, food and shelter, he belongs to a section
of mankind that orientate itself more "freely", that is, as an
independent existence. This, at once, makes him more-than-
animal, but also opens for the emergence of disruptive
desires. In the psychoanalysis of Jacques Lacan, human need
is always inscribed within the symbolic order. Thus, when
a baby's cry is interpreted as the expression of a need, the cry
comes to signify the demand of an other: the baby's cry
orientates a breast or a flask towards its mouth. Demand, in
this sense, brings need into a symbolic universe and articulates it with care and power. According to Lacan, desire on
the other hand is "neither the appetite for satisfaction, nor
the demand for love, but the difference that results from the
subtraction of the first from the second, the phenomenon
of their splitting (Spaltung)".[14] Desire, thus, moves us beyond
mere need, and tends to make itself infinite. Because desire
bears no essential relation to need, it allows for the orientation
of a subject beyond what it was, towards the risk of death.
Also Robinson partakes in this narrativisation of desire as the
path of death, both when he speaks of his brother, and
when he describes his own desire as casting him "down again

46

14   Lacan, 1977 [1959], Écrits: A Selection. London: Tavistock,
pp. 286-7.

into the deepest gulf of human misery that ever man fell into, or perhaps could be consistent with life and a state of health in the world" (RC 43).

Desire is productive, rather than reproductive, constructive rather than generative, a vector rather than a circle, cultural rather than natural. If animal need is profoundly ecological, the modern privatized conception of desire – with the whole familiar Oedipal setup – folds back onto need, and makes it recursive, private, limited to the home, family or individ- ual, as that the need that must be satisfied to enable individ- ualised desire. From the perspective of individual desire, need is rendered as the needs of an individual. Both desire and need are orientated towards objects, rather than with- in relations of care and desire. Based on these abstract deter- minations of need and desire, we can develop the following rudimentary graphs:

(1)

Need returns to itself, and desire pushes beyond

(2)

When need is strong, desire tends to becomes weak or dreaming

The individual form of Robinson's break with patriarchal oppression, is clearly made possible by his secure station of life, which provides him with the minimal capital that gives him access to the displacing colonial capital flows, which al- lows him to break free as an entrepreneurial subject. For Defoe, this path of desire is intertwined with the risk of death, and the abandonment of the straight path of reason, which is defined in terms of the material and symbolic securi- ty of the home. Thus

> ...my ill fate pushed me on now with an obsti- nacy that nothing could resist; and though I had several times loud calls from my reason and my more composed judgment to go home, yet I had no power to do it. I know not what to call this, nor will I urge that it is a secret

overruling decree, that hurries us on to be
the instruments of our own destruction, even
though it be before us, and that we rush
upon it with our eyes open. (RC 14)

We catch a glimpse of the ideal organisation of desire within
Robinson's family (3) in the references to his father's advice,
in which desire becomes sedentary. And Robinson's ventures
into the world provide us with a very different graph of
desire in which individuals who are responsible for their own
reproduction join around a shared aim, in the form of a
business venture (4):

(3)

Convergence of
individual autonomy without
interdependence of need:

(4)

Symbiotic need and inter-
wined desire:

Orientated by a desire for wealth beyond his station,
Robinson took to sea, established a plantation in Brazil and
found himself a slave merchant off the West African coast.
Yet Robinson's narrative is also a narrative of colonial ex-
peditions gone awry. This drift perfectly mirrors the passage
from the secure patriarchal existence of the British bourgeoisie into a more aggressive colonial phase. This early part
of the novel forms a clear contrast to the central part on
the island, in as much as it describes the world of colonial
adventurism as contingent and violent, and irrationally
and destructively at odds with the patriarchal order. Like the
biblical Jonah, to whom he is at one point compared (RC 15),
Robinson's defiance of the father ends up with a shipwreck. But contrary to the familiar moralism that Defoe affirms,
Robinson does not return like the prodigal son to the
communion at the family table. Instead, like a lucky rather
than chosen Noah, he is allowed to build the world anew after

the waters have swallowed up the past. Thus, the central part of the book, the rational fiction celebrated by Rousseau as a pedagogical masterpiece, is interested in the methodical construction of a world on Robinson's island, and Robinson's own moral self-critique of the pride and excessive desire of his early years plays a big part of the inner monologue on the island. Here Robinson will no longer be subject to the play of necessity and contingency, between the necessities of the patriarchal family and the contingencies of the flows of globalising colonial capital, but a subject in charge of his own slowly accelerating powers of accumulation.

REMAINING ONESELF WITHOUT OTHERS

The heart of Robinson's narrative is, of course, his years on the island, after a tempest has swallowed up the rest of the crew on Robinson's ship and blown him ashore, alone on an unknown beach. Like a confused Noah that hasn't been warned of the impending flood, Robinson lands in a pristine land, void of sin and people. In the first moment of pro-found disorientation on the beach, Robinson is nonetheless orientated, as his body cries for food and water. A body, alone, orientated by its need to obtain the necessities of life. The stock of capital salvaged from the ship – food, arms, clothes, munition and tools – saves Robinson from a destiny as hunter-gatherer on the island, and equips him to take nature into his possession in a gentlemanly fashion. Defoe continues to describe the orientation of Robinson's movements in terms of need and desire: "… I had no need to be venturous, for I had no want of food, and of that which was very good too".[15] Yet, as he writes elsewhere, "… I had a great desire to make a more perfect discovery of the island, and to see what other productions I might find, which I yet knew nothing of".[16] Drawing on the bourgeois and colonial techniques he brought with him, his human capital as it were, he begins to map the island, and write an inventory

15   RC 128.
16   RC 115, Emphasis added.

of his possessions and the natural resources at hand, fortifying himself, and exploring and mapping the island. Robinson relates to the world as resource and possession, not as ecology. As Gilles Deleuze notes in 'Desert Island', instead of creating a new form of life, Robinson reconstitutes everyday bourgeois life from his little reserve of capital.[17] And in this situation, he eventually establishes himself a comfort rather like that of his middle station, in which his desires are productive rather than hyperbolic, and in which his needs are satisfied:

> From this moment I began to conclude in my mind that it was possible for me to be more happy in this forsaken, solitary condition than it was probable I should ever have been in any other particular state in the world; and with this thought I was going to give thanks to God for bringing me to this place. (RC 133)

This condition reminds us of the patriarchal sovereignty of the Englishman in his home, and indeed we can apply the word sovereignty here. As Jean-Jacques Rousseau argues, Robinson's kingdom can be understood as a model form of sovereignty:

> In any case, there can be no doubt that Adam was sovereign of the world, as Robinson Crusoe was of his island, as long as he was its only inhabitant; and this empire had the advantage that the monarch, safe on his throne, had no rebellions, wars, or conspirators to fear.[18]

This sovereignty is not the sovereignty over other men, but the dominion over the word's beasts and plants. Just as Rousseau forgets to mention Eve – is he subsuming her within Adam's household? – Robinson's island might remind us of the ancient Greek oikos, in which women, slaves and children were not considered persons. Yet Robinson's condition is more radical, he lives in absolute solitude in a paradisiacal world

17   Gilles Deleuze, Desert Islands: And Other Texts, 1953–1974 (MIT Press, 2004), 12.
18   Rousseau, The Social Contract, Book 1, Sec.2.

without relational, let alone political or sexual tension. Not only are references to concrete women absent in the island narrative, women do not even appear in the form of an absence, as missed or remembered. It is paradise before the creation of Eve, that male fantasy of bliss. The one point woman is mentioned it is in the form of a revealing analogy, describing the last remaining concern that Robinson has, the reproductive care for himself. While the reproductive efforts of Robinson could open towards a becoming-woman, this possibility is only revealed negatively, when he compares his failed attempt to make pottery, to the way "children make dirt pies, or as a woman would make pies that never learned to raise paste." Jacques Derrida remarks that the world of the book "is a world without sexual difference and without desire, without obvious sexual concern as such", but we might generalise this, and say without concern for the other, in so far as concern denotes a care for the other, whether human or natural.[19] As Michel Tournier writes in Friday, his rewriting the Robinson myth:

> …For all of us the presence of other people is a powerful element of distraction, not only because they constantly break into our activities and interrupt our trains of thought, but because the mere possibility of their doing so illuminates a world of concerns situated at the edge of our consciousness, but capable at any moment of becoming its centre.[20]

For Deleuze, the meaning of a Robinsonade – both Tournier's and Defoe's – is simply this: A world without others.[21] In his analysis of Friday, Gilles Deleuze argues that this solitude must necessarily lead to a radical erasure of Robinson's sense of self, to his "dehumanization".[22] Without others, there is no one to confirm a shared horizon of possibility, and

19   Derrida, The Beast and the Sovereign, 93.
20   Michael Tournier, Friday, or the Other Island
(Pantheon, 1985), 360.
21   Gilles Deleuze, The Logic of Sense, ed. Constantin V. Boundas,
trans. Mark Lester and Charles Stivale, 0 ed. (Columbia University
Press, 1990), 319.
22   Ibid., 303.

without others the Other – the symbolic order – starts to fall apart. This would then throw the individual into a profound state of disorientation, and expose it to the world without a schema of meaning. Deleuze's text becomes a radical inquiry into desubjectivation. Yet, unlike Tournier's Robinson, Defoe's does not become radically decentred. Instead, living without others and the need to care, Robinson enters a state of paradisiacal bliss. This blissful male is blissful because he lives without concern for the others that masculinity normally defines itself in opposition to, and which define and render the male ego unstable and not-all. Robinson's early sovereignty is that of a strangely pre-political world without subjects or enemies. But is this simply a result of refusal on Defoe's part, to think through the radical consequences of living in a world without others, a kind of fantasy of solid-ity that cannot, by definition, be realised? Certainly, Defoe is aware that Robinson must linger at the edge of madness, or as James Joyce has noted that Defoe's characters are "reaching in two directions, backwards towards their animal origins and forward to their roles as historic prototypes".[23] Indeed there is something animalistic in Robinson's sover-eignty, which bears a certain semblance to Georges Bataille's beastly concept of sovereignty, according to which "What is sovereign in fact is to enjoy the present time without having anything else in view but this present time".[24] The answer to why Defoe's Robinson does not become dehumanized like Tournier's, we have to understand its other side, where it touches on a historical prototype, the heroic individual.[25]

23   James Joyce quoted in chapter 4, note 7 of Robert James Merrett, Daniel Defoe, Contrarian (University of Toronto Press, 2013).
24   Georges Bataille, The Accursed Share, Vols. 2 and 3: The History of Eroticism and Sovereignty, trans. Robert Hurley, Reprint edition (New York: Zone Books, 1993), 199.
25   In an autobiographical note, Freud expresses this strange bourgeois combination of comfort and heroism in a pure form: "…like Robinson Crusoe, I settled down as comfortably as possible on my desert island. When I look back on those lonely years, away from the pressures and confusions of today, it seems like a glorious heroic age. My 'splendid isolation' was not without its advantages and charms. I did not have to read any publications, nor listen to any ill-informed opponents; I was not subject to influence from any quarter; there was nothing to hustle me". Sigmund Freud and Carrie Lee Rothgeb, The Standard Edition of the Complete Psycho-logical Works of Sigmund Freud: On the History of Psycho-Analytic Movement, Papers on Metapsychology and Other Works (Hogarth Press and the Institute of Psycho-Analysis, 1957), 22.

As we have seen, Robinson's individualism has a specific-ally calculative character, and obsession with raising himself above the immanence of beastly existence. With reference to Max Weber's thesis on the protestant work ethic and the origins of the spirit of capitalism, Deleuze points out that Robinson's efforts are given meaning within a protestant logic of providence according to which "God knows his people, the hardworking honest type, by their beautiful properties, and the evil doers, by their poorly maintained, shabby proper-ty".[26] While Robinson does not partake in a social teleology of capitalist accumulation, he can interpret his private success as a sign of God's providence. His tribulations were all for the better, not because he was saved from the island (this would merely return him to the starting point), but because they brought Robinson closer to God and into the possession of the island. Without this theological horizon, Robinson's private labours would take him no further than the mere me-chanical existence of the poor, proto-animal part of humanity or the circular, reproductive activity imposed on women.

But perhaps we should reverse Max Weber's theory here, which sees protestant theology as a belief that gives mean-ing and legitimacy to the private everyday labour of accumula-tion. To be in a world without others reverses the Weberian narrative. The latter shows how, within a community of believers, religion can be the spiritual foundation of everyday practice, because it is the social code that sanctions indi-vidual behaviour. But without such a community and its ritu-als, religion becomes abstract thought spinning on its own. That is, unless everyday practices – such as methodical labour, accounting, and time keeping – become rituals sustain-ing religion. In other words, Robinson does not merely believe in order to give meaning and direction to his work, nor does he work merely to survive: He works in order to sus-tain his belief, which is what keeps his symbolic world from disintegrating. Thus the measured, persistent efforts to optimize everyday activity becomes a condition of orientation, a way through which the isolated individual keeps mad-ness at bay. Well aware of the risks of circularity or psychotic

53

26   Deleuze, Desert Islands, 12.

swerving that the cogito opens up, René Descartes had already shown in 1637, that the individual must be firm and methodical in its actions to avoid the problem circularity opened up by individuality, or metaphorically by island life, where the straight path eventually becomes circular. According to Descartes one must imitate

> travellers who, finding themselves lost in some forest, should not wander about turning this way or that, nor, worse still, stop in one place, but should always walk in as straight a line as they can...[27]

Robinson's theology gives him the straight path, and book keeping, calculation, exploration, cartography, production, etc., constitute the practical, methodical stride that escapes madness. Kant would later, in 1786, make the "practical need" for "rational belief" constitutive of his concept of orientation. [28] When orientation becomes an individual feat, the other as distraction soon becomes a threat not merely to the bliss, but to the sanity of the individual.

THE OTHER
BETWEEN ANXIETY
AND SUBJECTION

When one day Robinson discovers footsteps in the sand as he circles the island, he is struck by panic and flees from the trace. Hiding in his den, anxiety engulfs him. Even Defoe knows that within this paradisiacal solitude, Robinson must remain haunted by the spectre of the other. Not too long before Defoe, Thomas Hobbes described the state of nature as a state of fear of the other, in which no recourse to contract or law is possible. Similarly for Robinson, despite his loneliness, the other is first of all a source of fear. If before, death was the necessary risk that came with pursuing his desires to go beyond middle class self-satisfaction, it now reappears as a

27   René Descartes and Donald A. Cress, Discourse on Method (Third Edition) (Hackett Publishing, 1998), 13.
28   Immanuel Kant, "What Is Orientation in Thinking?," in Political Writings, trans. H.B. Nesbit, 2nd ed. (Cambridge: Cambridge University Press, 1990), 237 – 49.

threat to his insular being, a threat of becoming reduced to a mechanical being, a human animal that might become the prey of cannibals. But since Robinson has no knowledge of the one that left the trace, his reaction must be understood as a paranoid fantasy. The other is not only a potential threat to his security, but much more radically, the mere trace of the other subverts his individual sovereignty. Worse than the concrete fear of a known other, the meeting with the traces of an unknown other provokes a profound disorientating anxiety in Robinson, "like a man perfectly confused and out of myself, I came home to my fortification, not feeling, as we say, the ground I went on, but terrified to the last degree", his imagination affected by "wild ideas" and "unaccountable whimsies", in a polymorphous search for a concrete threat which could focalise the anxiety into fear. Like Descartes' solipsistic cogito which fears it has been fooled by a demon, the solitary Robinson passes from a state of absolute security to absolute scepticism: might the devil himself have imprinted the naked foot on the sand? For Robinson, the trace of the other is sublime; overwhelming and unsettling, it pushes his imagination to its limits, into a state of pain.

Torn out of his everyday rituals, Robinson cannot confirm God and be confirmed, but instead God becomes a vengeful sovereign, punishing Crusoe for his sins. While he reports finding some consolation in religion, it provides no answer to his anxiety. The decentring concern produced by the other, is only removed by a negation of the other. Robinson finally settles for a theory that is commensurate with his insular subjectivity: the footstep must be his own, reencountered after walking full circle. Like Kant notes with respect to the sublime, the pleasure of the sublime is not given with the character of the object, but is produced by the mind itself in order to compensate for this pain. The disorientation caused by the sublime leads to a turning inwards to subjectivity. The evil of natural catastrophe (or of mathematical regress) is reversed into an occasion for the celebration of the good of human dignity and reason.[29] The absence of beauty and

29   Gene Ray, "Reading the Lisbon Earthquake: Adorno, Lyotard, and the Contemporary Sublime," The Yale Journal of Criticism 17, no. 1 (2004): 9, doi:10.1353/yale.2004.0007.

purpose itself has a purpose: turning man towards his own inner teleology.

However, the damage to Robinson's self-enclosed security is done, and his mode of being changes radically:

> In my reflections upon the state of my case since I came on shore on this island, I was comparing the happy posture of my affairs in the first years of my habitation here, with the life of anxiety, fear, and care which I had lived in ever since I had seen the print of a foot in the sand (RC 232).

The anxiety provoked by the unknown other is stronger than the fear provoked by concrete others. A concrete other transforms the anxiety into a contest of cunning and strength. We see this when he finally encounters a troop of cannibals, and helps the man he calls Friday escape The cannibals constitute a clear enemy and a concrete threat and Friday is no true other who could threaten Robinson's sovereign kingdom. Instead, the encounter with both constitutes the beginning of the transformation of Robinson's sovereignty from a simple state of nature sovereignty to a proto-monarchical sovereignty. Starting from the claim of possession of a territory, we will see that others entering, even those that are not racialized, must be transformed into subjects or enemies, just as visitors to even the most generous hosts become enemies, if they do not respect the host's dominion of his premises.

Robinson easily makes Friday a subject, because he is too servile to be an enemy or a rebellious voice like Shakespeare's Caliban (with whom Defoe was familiar). In fact, Crusoe approaches Friday first as dog salvaged from a violent owner, then as a child, and Defoe lets Friday interpellate him as his absolute master. For Robinson this encounter is without anxiety, because in his arrogance and ignorance he (and his author) see only a "savage" without a name, someone to convert and christen. Friday is no Caliban, both because he desires submission but also because he can be symbolically inscribed into Robinson's world as a fellow if subaltern Protestant. Thus Robinson's pre-political kingdom is transformed into a political kingdom, with enemies – the cannibals – and a subject.

Friday learns much from Robinson – "he was the aptest scholar that ever was" – yet he remains a servant; like Kant's "roher Mensch" it does not seem that Defoe thinks it is within his nature to be able to go through a process of education, Bildung, by which he could learn to become an autonomous subject.[30] The obvious objection to this racist argument, of course, is that the problem is not Friday's ability to learn, but that his racialization and dispossession means that he cannot be recognized as an autonomous subject within the occidental "civilizational" paradigm.

Robinson's relation to the Spanish sailors who later arrive on the island is starkly different. He fears them as potential enemies, but ultimately lets them become his subjects under condition that their captain signs a contract leaving all claims of sovereignty to Robinson. Yet care must be taken not to reduce Friday to a victim of exclusion from a realm of contract and universality, which we would thereby confirm as an ultimate telos of humanity. Might there not be something in Friday that resists becoming an "autonomous subject"? Might we, without romanticising Friday as a noble savage, suggest that he knows ways of satisfying his needs and pursuing his desires that do not entail submission to the paradigm of possessive individualism? Creating a counter-fictional narrative of the ontology and subjectivity of Friday is a question of our capacity to imagine an overcoming of the Robinsons within us, to the point of following Deleuze in saying that "any healthy reader would dream of seeing him [Friday] eat Robinson".[31] This is the value of Michel Tournier's novel and Deleuze's essay on it.[32] Tournier presents Friday as Robinson's shamanic guide, a relation made possible only because Robinson has been radically dehumanised by his years of solitude. In these examples, the overcoming of Robinsonian man is conditioned on a radical erasure. Rather than an alternative answer to the

30   Gayatri Chakravorty Spivak, A Critique of Postcolonial Reason (Cambridge, Mass: Harvard University Press, 1999), 13.
31   Deleuze, Desert Islands, 12.
32   Tournier, Friday, or the Other Island; Deleuze, The Logic of Sense.

problem of disorientation in displacement, we find here a radical dissolution of the problem through an affirmation of disorientation or the cannibal consumption of the displaced individual. The eating of Robinson is a valid political proposition when he is seen as the prototypical colonialist or an ideological fiction. But this fails to understand that Robinson is not merely an agent of violence, obfuscation and legitimation, but an answer to a persistent problem of displacement. The task then becomes to think different answers to this problem, not merely negating one of its solutions. The point here is both to engage the disorientating challenge indigenous life and thought poses to European self-understanding and subverting Robinson's claim to be the universal representative of Europe. This can be done by returning to a counter-history of west-ward migration from Europe in sources that Defoe knew well but ignored.

ORIENTATING ONESELF
WITH CANNIBALS

Below Robinson's middle state, there existed and exists a subterranean strata of subjectivities in Europe, which in many ways were submitted to a process of internal colonization and expropriation, even as some of them were becoming enrolled in the European colonization of the rest of the world. Through a brief encounter with these hewers of wood and draws of water, so beautifully brought to our memory by Peter Linebaugh and Marcus Rediker, another conception of orientation might open up.[33] Like Robinson's this conception is an answer to modern displacement, but one which undermines possessive individualism as the privileged centre of orientation. Let's look at another kind of story of shipwrecks and stranding: those of the Sea-Venture and the Bounty for example.

In 1609, some fifty years before the fictional character Robinson stranded on his Caribbean island, an English ship bound for the new colony of Virginia, sailed into a terrible

58

conditions

33   Peter Linebaugh and Marcus Rediker, The Many-Headed Hydra:
The Hidden History of the Revolutionary Atlantic (Verso Books, 2002).

tempest. Leaking and creaking in a three-day storm, the Sea-Venture and its crew seemed doomed to go under. Antic-ipating equality in death, the men and women aboard cracked open the casks and "'drunk one to the other" without regard for station or rank. But with a luck greater than Robinson's, the ship wrecked on the island of Bermuda without loss of life. Like so many marooned slaves and commoners before and after them, the men and women of the Sea-Venture set about living life in common on the island, collecting and pro-ducing what they needed. These did not come as Robinson with the existing social relations of England only inscribed on their inside, these also existed between them. But most of the shipwrecked were from the supposedly "mechanical" part of humanity, and they thus rebelled against the re-impositions of strict labour by their former superiors.[34] In many colonies black slaves and white European proletarians plot-ted rebellions together, while their masters tried to separated them with the imposition of racial hierarchies.[35] This is but a few examples of a historical possibility that escapes Defoe and all the readers who have taken his Robinson as a para-digmatic figure. Or perhaps this possibility did not so much elude Defoe as it was repressed in his writing of Robinson Crusoe (and thus also in the many immanent critiques of the book). Yet, as David Rediker has shown, Defoe was very well versed in the narratives of pirates and sailors, and he must have been aware that many stranded seamen only sur-vived through collaboration with one another and with the indigenous inhabitants where they stranded.[36]

Such ideas were also present in the literature of the pre-ceding two centuries, from Thomas More's Utopia (1516) and Michel de Montaigne's Of Cannibals (1580) to Shakespeare's The Tempest (1611), all of which served as inspirations for Robinson Crusoe. Both Montaigne and More drew upon oral tales from mariners who had visited the new world, and Shakespeare wrote his play upon learning of the story of the Sea-Venture. Shakespeare, despite being himself of the

34   Ibid., 30.
35   Silvia Federici, Caliban and the Witch: Women, the Body and Primitive Accumulation (Autonomedia, 2004), 107.
36   Rediker, Outlaws of the Atlantic, 75.

middle class and an investor in the colonial adventures of the Virginia Company, showed a sense of the struggles and aspirations of the commoners that are absent in Robinson Crusoe. The Tempest plays out after the protagonist Prospero, the "rightful" duke of Milan, is exiled on an island only inhabited by the rebellious Caliban and the spirit Ariel, who he takes as a loyal servant. In the play we find a moving speech by the king's adviser Gonzalo:

> I' th' commonwealth I would, by contraries,
> Execute all things; for no kind of traffic
> Would I admit; no name of magistrate;
> Letters should not be known; riches, poverty,
> And use of service, none;
> contract, succession,
> Bourn, bound of land, tilth, vineyard, none;
> No use of metal, corn, or wine, or oil;
> No occupation, all men idle, all;
> And women too, but innocent and pure;
> No sovereignty –– [37]

Gonzalo's discourse, like Montaigne's and More's, would have certainly resonated with the English commoners who in the 16 and 17th centuries were going through the first big process of dispossession. But the three conceptions are vastly different. Where More and Montaigne directly present their utopias as based on experience, Shakespeare's lets a royal advisor, Gonzalo, express a colonial fantasy: "Had I plantation of this isle... And were the king on't, what would I do?". In the play, the king's brother Sebastian immediately subverts Gonzalo's "no sovereignty" by sarcastically reminding him: "Yet he would be king on't" (II.i.152). In 1969 Aime Césaire's anti-colonial renarration of Shakespeare's play A Tempest would draw out the implications of Gonzalo's unwillingness to let the "savages" challenge that Europe, which Césaire just after the second world war had pointed out was "morally, spiritually indefensible".[38]

37   William Shakespeare, The Tempest: Evans Shakespeare Edition, ed. Grace Tiffany (Cengage Learning, 2011), 91; II.i.148 – 157.
38   Aimé Césaire, Discourse on Colonialism (NYU Press, 2001), 32.

I mean that if the island is inhabited, as I believe, and if we colonize it, as is my hope, then we have to take every precaution not to import our shortcomings, yes, what we call civilization. They must stay as they are: savages, noble and good savages, free, without any complexes or complications. Something like a pool granting eternal youth where we periodically come to restore our aging, citified souls.[39]

Thus Gonzalo's position of enunciation betrays the falseness of his discourse, and points us in the direction of a critique of charity. To defend the authenticity of the colonized without challenging the coloniality of the relation amounts to maintaining dominion in the guise of paternalistic charity. This can be pushed in the direction of the Manichean conflict between colonizer and colonized whereby the desire for the colonized to eat their colonizers appear not as an affirmation of the authentic savagery of the colonised, but as the turning of the cannibalism of colonialism against the colonizers.[40] If the destruction of colonialism requires the clarification of antagonism, the problem of inventing different solutions to displacement requires the exploration of different relations to the other. Here it will be productive to look at the relation between indigenous and Europeans in the fluid state, prior to the crystallisation of this relation into a Manichean opposition. The aim is not to impose a category of universal humanity in order to show the sameness of the two, but to investigate a space of composition between or beyond the antagonistic poles of the colonised and the colonizer – to proliferate rather than negate their difference.

Shakespeare had taken the passage almost ad verbatim from Montaigne's essay, which in turn was based on the oral accounts of a man, most likely a servant, within

39   Aimé Césaire, A Tempest, trans. Richard Miller (New York: Ubu Repertory Theater Publications, 1985), 24.
40   Such Manichean anti-colonialism was famously affirmed at the beginning of Frantz Fanon Wretched of the Earth, while the nuances he introduced later in that book – the militant white anti-colonialist, the opportunistic and corrupted black leader, etc. – are often forgotten. Frantz Fanon, The Wretched of the Earth, 1st Evergreen Black Cat Edition (New York: Grove Press, 1968).

Montaigne's household. He had "lived ten or twelve years in the New World", including with the cannibals of the Amazon. Montaigne describes this man as a "plain ignorant fellow", too simple to lie in order to gain "the reputation of men of judgment".[41] Yet his keen observations suggest that he is not as stupid as Montaigne suggest, but rather unlearned and uninterested in inventing evidence to satisfy the prejudices of his master. If we strip Montaigne's text of its suffocating classical references, which serve to create a common measure between Europeans and the cannibals, and put the latter in a favourable light, we see the contours of an oral history, told by a common man born in France. This man's narrative does not display Crusoe's colonial gaze upon the other, but rather testifies to an engagement. It is rather an example of a kind of lay anthropology, in a sense that comes close to Eduardo Viveiros de Castro's thesis

> that every non-trivial anthropological theory is a version of an indigenous practice of knowledge, all such theories being situatable in strict structural continuity with the intellectual pragmatics of the collectives that historically occupied the position of object in the discipline's gaze.[42]

Long before to this call to decolonize the discipline of anthropology, Montaigne's essay documents a transatlantic encounter that refused to reduce difference to human sameness or the affirmation of a chasm. Montaigne was writing at the times of the European wars of religion, during which the rebels of Münster and Mühlhausen affirmed the communist slogan: Omnia Sunt Communia. Montaigne, who found himself at the court of Charles IX in Rouen, met three Brazilian cannibals, who noted the vast inequalities of French society, its two halves, and "they thought it strange

41   Michel de Montaigne and George Savile Marquis of Halifax, Montaigne's Essays in Three Books: With Notes and Quotations. And an Account of the Author's Life. With a Short Character of the Author and Translator (B. and B. Barker, 1743), 227.
42   Eduardo Viveiros de Castro, "Cannibal Metaphysics: Amerindian Perspectivism," Radical Philosophy 182 (December 2013): 18, http://www.radicalphilosophy.com/article/cannibal-metaphysics-amerindian-perspectivism.

that these necessitous halves were able to suffer so great
an inequality and injustice, and that they did not take the others
by the throats, or set fire to their houses".[43]

The texts of Montaigne, More and Shakespeare show
that in narrating the disorientating encounter with the "New
World" an non-Robinsonian orientation was available to
Defoe, a pragmatics of dealing with displacement that did not
entail possessiveness, sovereignty and racialized enmity.
This is also the case of the oral histories of the commoners of
the Sea-Venture, and their rebellion against the return of
hierarchical command and the fierce labour of the Virginia
Company. Their orientation was that of embodied desires
and needs to create lives in common, without masters.[44] While
these commoners did not abide to the hierarchical world
view of Crusoe, we do not know if they would have shared his
colonial thirst of submitting the inhabitants of Bermuda
had it been inhabited. Yet, we do know that many displaced
English commoners, who had for centuries been colonised
by the lords and the centralising state and expropriated by the
enclosures, desired a form of life not too different from the
life of the inhabitants of the Caribbean islands. Throughout the
colonisation process, escaped slaves and indentured
servants from Europe escaped the colonies to live among the
indigenous or to form their own maroon communities.
Such escapes were subject to fierce punishments and often
death at the hands of the colonial authorities.[45] This was
the case for the sailors who mutinied on the HMS Bounty on
the 28 of April 1789 in the Pacific Ocean, less than three
months before the people of Paris stormed the Bastille. The
Bounty, as told by Linebaugh and Rediker, was on a

> planetary voyage to... to collect food (bread-
> fruit) from the pacific to feed people imported
> from Africa who slaved on West Indian plan-
> tations, where they made sugar to provide
> empty calories for the proletarians in Europe.[46]

43   Montaigne and Halifax, Montaigne's Essays in Three Books, 239.
44   Linebaugh and Rediker, The Many-Headed Hydra, 21.
45   Cedric J. Robinson, Black Movements in America (Routledge,
2013), chapter 1; Robert Chaudenson, Creolization of Language
and Culture (Routledge, 2002), 87.
46   Linebaugh and Rediker, The Many-Headed Hydra, 277.

Usually the story of the mutiny is told as a story about rebellion against the unjust Captain Bligh, but this forgets that the men of the Bounty only rebelled after having spent five months among the Tahitians, forming many relationships with them, and experiencing a mode of life quite different from the poverty they knew from home and the harsh discipline that was universal in the British navy. After the munity, the men of the Bounty settled among the inhabitants of Tahiti without any project of conquest.[47] Ultimately, the British navy returned to persecute them, but they managed to escape to the remote pacific island of Pitcairn, where they founded a desperately poor commune with a number of Tahitians who came with them. This commune exists to this day, despite the fierce difficulties experienced by its isolated inhabitants.

More often than not, the orientations of mutinous sailors and commoners were not orientated by ideas of the particular historical destiny of a people or by the universal history of humanity. If at all relating to such notions, they were on a line of flight both from the emerging "nations" at home and from the globalising machine that was imposing a certain vision of humanity through missionaries, gunboats and small pox. These imagined communities were of minor importance compared to the lines of flight produced by the displacements created by the colonial state and capitalism. In the case of many of the sailors and migrants on the Sea-Venture, their movements must be understood as extensions – sometimes forced – of the migration created by the enclosures, while Robinson's free enterprising must be connected to the privateering merchant capitalism tolerated and sometimes promoted by the British crown in the 17th and 18th century. The mutinous sailors and commoners did not simply decide to autonomously pursue a line of flight, but to engage differently with the "objective" lines of flight, the displacement created by nascent capitalism and primitive accumulation. They did so by combining in a common struggle and life within their displacement, which also allowed them to compose with many non-European populations.

47   Ibid., 353a.

ROBINSON BEYOND IDEOLOGY AND IDEOLOGY CRITIQUE

Today, in a world where almost all land is the property of someone and most commons have been expropriated or subsumed by capital, the orientational horizon for the movement of the displaced is profoundly altered. There are no desert islands, but we might begin to speak of the global island of capital. The sources of displacement today are many, and take the form of forces overflowing us or pulling us along, as well our own desires to move and change. It remains the case, however, that displacement is profoundly individualising, severing not only the familiar patriarchal power relations, but also the bonds of care and commoning that were there or might have been developing. In some sense, Robinson Crusoe seems almost naïve as a dispositive of orientation today, because it shows immediately what we only live in mediated ways. Robinson reduces his ecologies to a set of resources, and others to trading partners, threats or servants. When we do the same today, we do so in ways that are mediated by the market and opaque political and juridical systems. In Marx's terms, Robinson's life is a life without fetishism, while ours is rife with it. But this naivety is also reason that Robinson Crusoe can be seen as a matrix for orientation within contemporary displacement: it proposes a subjective relation to displacement, according to which displacement is not a misfortune and a loss of relationship, but an opportunity of a true self-relationship, in which the subject realises its full and hitherto unknown abilities through unalienated labour, discovery and conquest, self-development and self-discipline. In the absence of other strategies of living and desiring within displacement like the ones that were once developed by mutineers and maroons, the Robinsonian orientation will continue to suggests itself as a way to navigate this displacement and stabilise ourselves as displaced individuals, and continue to be a way to avoid disorientation, anxiety and the early individual death – mental or bodily – that always becomes a risk when relations of care and reproduction are severed.

My reading of Robinson Crusoe started from the idea that the book inaugurates the construction of modern, western male subjectivity, both as a literary expression of a profound historical shift in the structure of feeling, and as a hugely influential technology of orientation, a dispositive for imagining and working on oneself. As such, we understand how Robinson Crusoe is not merely a modern myth or an ideological trope. To understand the significance of Robinson on this level, it has to be related to the pragmatics of orientation, beyond two classical interpretations of the Robinson myth: firstly the liberal appropriation of the myth as a mediation of the nature of the homo oeconomicus, and secondly, the classical critique of Robinson as a reflection of the particularisms of European bourgeois ideology. Both focus on the fact that Robinson reproduced the orientation of his society when he landed on the island, and the fact that he didn't create something truly new.

The first explanation of this fact is taken as a proof of the innate naturalness of Robinson's orientation. Thus the Robinson myth is interpreted as a thought experiment which mirrors the isolated experiments that scientists were developing at the time. This experiment is supposed to demonstrate how the natural propensities of man emerge in splendid isolation. Thus the novel can be understood as a rational Ur-myth of economic man. The second explanation shows that Robinson's long discourses on repentance show that he stands at the brink between a backward-looking Protestantism and a forward-looking capitalism, at the overlap of the protestant work ethic and the spirit of capitalism. For this reading it is easy to dismiss the idea of Robinson as a true thought experiment. There was no rupture when Robinson landed on the island, he straight-forwardly reproduced the social relations and attitudes he knew from home. Thus the ideological character of the first reading can be revealed by showing how it rests on a continuity in the mode of production, or by reference to Robinson's class or nationality.

Both interpretations ultimately fail because they don't consider the contingency that marks out displacement. The interpretation that sees Robinson Crusoe as an expression of human nature fails because it over-stresses the rupture of the shipwreck in order to see any continuity as a necessary expression of innate traits. Reversely, the interpretation that sees the book as a document of the protestant work ethic fails because it ends up with a concept of innate orientation, not as a matter of nature, but of class and national background. The first reading too readily universalises the Robinsonian subjectivity, the other particularises it too fast as essentially middle class or English. These narratives of continuity both pose the question of displacement in relation to disorientation, and the way in which it introduces contingency into orientation.

THE CHALLENGE
IT IS NOT TO BECOME
ROBINSON

Orientation, of course, has to do with both what a body-mind can do, and what it has learned socially. Yet, when we are dealing with situations of contingency and displacement we must understand the primacy of the pragmatic and existential question of orientation. Robinson's mapping, calculation, theology, constructions of fences and weapons, etc., are pragmatic and existential tools of bodily and mental orientation. Now it becomes possible to see why Robinson repeated the orientational strategies of his station British society. He did so because these strategies which he has learned and accepted at home were possible, effective and in some sense necessary as survival strategies in his isolation on the island. Had Robinson landed on the island without supply, and had he been taken in and cared for by Friday's family, his reorientation would not have taken the form of a return or continuity. He might have seen Friday as a fellow commoner and the island as an ecology rather than a collection of resources.

The point is not to excuse or condemn Robinson for being ideological or a product of his environment, but to understand how orientation is related to practical and existential strategies and tactics of life. These are ways to satisfy needs and construct or pursue desires. The simple negation of these strategies would result in disorientation or debilitating anxiety, and ultimately death. As such they are not universally human, nor essentially English or middle class. Robinson Crusoe relies on the reader's ability to empathise with Robinson's separation from others, and the practical problems he faces, as well as the pleasure he takes from his own labour and autonomy. Robinson Crusoe can be and has been taken up far beyond its narrow cultural horizon not because it articulates an essentially human condition, but because it speaks to an experience of separation, which has become generalised through capitalist colonization and globalisation, and because it provides one seemingly desirable and practical way of constituting a stout and capable individuality in that condition of separation. This is the problem that we have in common with Robinson, and the reason the form of the Robinson narrative remains alive.

This also means that the Robinsonian orientation cannot be destroyed through critique alone. Because it is not simply an ideology it can only be replaced by the development of other practical and existential strategies and tactics of life, that is different, compositive ways of living displacement or by an abolition of displacement. No desire to overcome separation will in itself produce more than a new identity, an imaginary "we" to pave over the distance that tends to reduce any care to a care of the self. Desires for a we will hollow and abstract unless they are connected to collective strategies and tactics of life, and struggles against the forces that separate, displace and thereby recreate the rituals that keep the Robinson myth alive.

Bibliography

conditions

Bataille, Georges. The Accursed Share, Vols. 2 and 3: The History of Eroticism and Sovereignty. Translated by Robert Hurley. Reprint edition. New York Zone Books, 1993.

Castro, Eduardo Viveiros de. "Cannibal Metaphysics: Amerindian Perspectivism." Radical Philosophy 182 (December 2013). http://www.radicalphilosophy.com/ article/cannibal-metaphysics-amerindian-perspectivism.

Césaire, Aimé. A Tempest. Translated by Richard Miller. New York: Ubu Repertory Theater Publications, 1985.

Césaire, Aimé. Discourse on Colonialism. NYU Press, 2001.

Chaudenson, Robert. Creolization of Language and Culture. Routledge, 2002.

Defoe, Daniel. The Life and Strange Surprizing Adventures of Robinson Crusoe, of York, Mariner: Who Lived Eight and Twenty Years All Alone in an Un-Inhabited Island on the Coast of America, Near the Mouth of the Great River of Oroonoque; Having Been Cast on Shore by Shipwreck, Wherein All the Men Perished But Himself: With an Account How He Was at Last as Strangely Deliver'd by Pyrates. Written by Himself. W. Taylor, 1719.

Deleuze, Gilles. Desert Islands: And Other Texts, 1953–1974. MIT Press, 2004.

Deleuze, Gilles. The Logic of Sense. Edited by Constantin V. Boundas. Translated by Mark Lester and Charles Stivale. 0 ed. Columbia University Press, 1990.

Deleuze, Gilles, and Felix Guattari. Anti-Oedipus: Capitalism and Schizophrenia. New Ed. London: Continuum, 2004.

Derrida, Jacques. The Beast and the Sovereign. University of Chicago Press, 2011.

Descartes, René, and Donald A. Cress. Discourse on Method (Third Edition). Hackett Publishing, 1998.

Fanon, Frantz. The Wretched of the Earth. 1st Evergreen Black Cat Edition. New York: Grove Press, 1968.

Federici, Silvia. Caliban and the Witch: Women, the Body and Primitive Accumulation. Autonomedia, 2004.

Freud, Sigmund, and Carrie Lee Rothgeb. The Standard Edition of the Complete Psychological Works of Sigmund Freud: On the History of Psycho-Analytic Movement, Papers on Metapsychology and Other Works. Hogarth Press and the Institute of Psycho-Analysis, 1957.

Guest, Kristen. Eating Their Words: Cannibalism and the Boundaries of Cultural Identity. SUNY Press, 2014.

Joyce, James. Occasional, Critical, and Political Writing. Edited by Kevin Barry and Conor Deane. Oxford University Press, 2000.

Kant, Immanuel. "What Is Orientation in Thinking?" In Political Writings, translated by H.B. Nesbit, 2nd ed., 237–49. Cambridge: Cambridge University Press, 1990.

Linebaugh, Peter, and Marcus Rediker. The Many-Headed Hydra: The Hidden History of the Revolutionary Atlantic. Verso Books, 2002.

Marx, Karl. Capital: Volume I. Translated by Ben Fowkes. London: Penguin Books, 1976.

Merrett, Robert James. Daniel Defoe, Contrarian. University of Toronto Press, 2013.

Montaigne, Michel de, and George Savile Marquis of Halifax. Montaigne's Essays in Three Books: With Notes and Quotations. And an Account of the Author's Life. With a Short Character of the Author and Translator. B. and B. Barker, 1743.

Ray, Gene. "Reading the Lisbon Earthquake: Adorno, Lyotard, and the Contemporary Sublime." The Yale Journal of Criticism 17, no. 1 (2004): 1–18. doi:10.1353/yale.2004.0007.

Rediker, Marcus. Outlaws of the Atlantic: Sailors, Pirates, and Motley Crews in the Age of Sail. Beacon Press, 2014.

Robinson, Cedric J. Black Movements in America. Routledge, 2013.

Severin, Tim. In Search Of Robinson Crusoe. Basic Books, 2009.

Shakespeare, William. The Tempest: Evans Shakespeare Edition. Edited by Grace Tiffany. Cengage Learning, 2011.

Spivak, Gayatri Chakravorty. A Critique of Postcolonial Reason. Cambridge, Mass: Harvard University Press, 1999.

Tournier, Michael. Friday, or the Other Island. Pantheon, 1985.

Watt, Ian. Myths of Modern Individualism: Faust, Don Quixote, Don Juan, Robinson Crusoe. Cambridge University Press, 1997.

Williams, Raymond. Keywords: A Vocabulary of Culture and Society. Routledge, 2011.

Williams, Raymond. "Structures of Feeling." In Marxism and Literature. Oxford: Oxford University Press, 1977.

Petrol
Series

by Manuela
Zechner

Peak displacement

Migration is when the door closes behind you

The number of people regitered
as 'displaced' by the UN has
never been as high as now since
world war II, and it keeps rising

As opposed to other civilizational crises, this is not about the collapse of a part of the population, nor of a concrete territory but a collapse that concerns the entire planet, where there are no more places to go

Peak displacement – petrol picture series
compiled by Manuela Zechner.

1.   'Peak displacement' follows peak oil.
Public Domain photo snatched
online.

2.   'Migration is when the door closes
behind you' is a collective thought of the
Precarity Office Vienna from one of their
sessions on migration, mobility and crisis.
Photo by Loco Steve from Orpington,
UK – The San Ardo Oil Field From The Coast
Starlight. CC BY 2.0 Wikimedia.

3.   'The number of people registered as
"displaced"[...]' my words, public domain
photo snatched online.

4.   'As opposed to other civilizational
crises, [...]' Words by Ramón Fernández
Durán y Luis González Reyes, in 'La Espiral
de la Energía'. http://www.ecologistas
enaccion.org/article29055.html

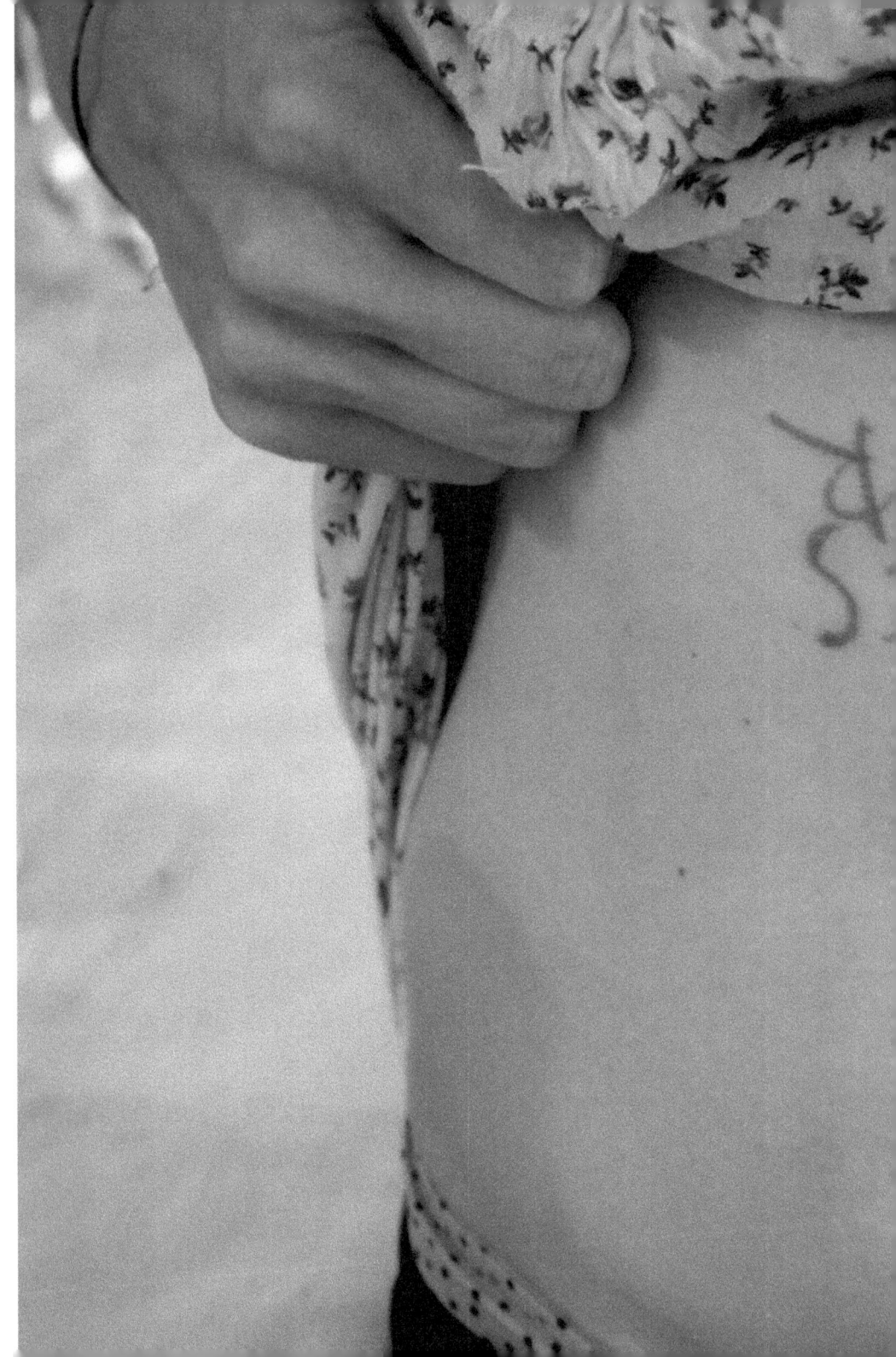

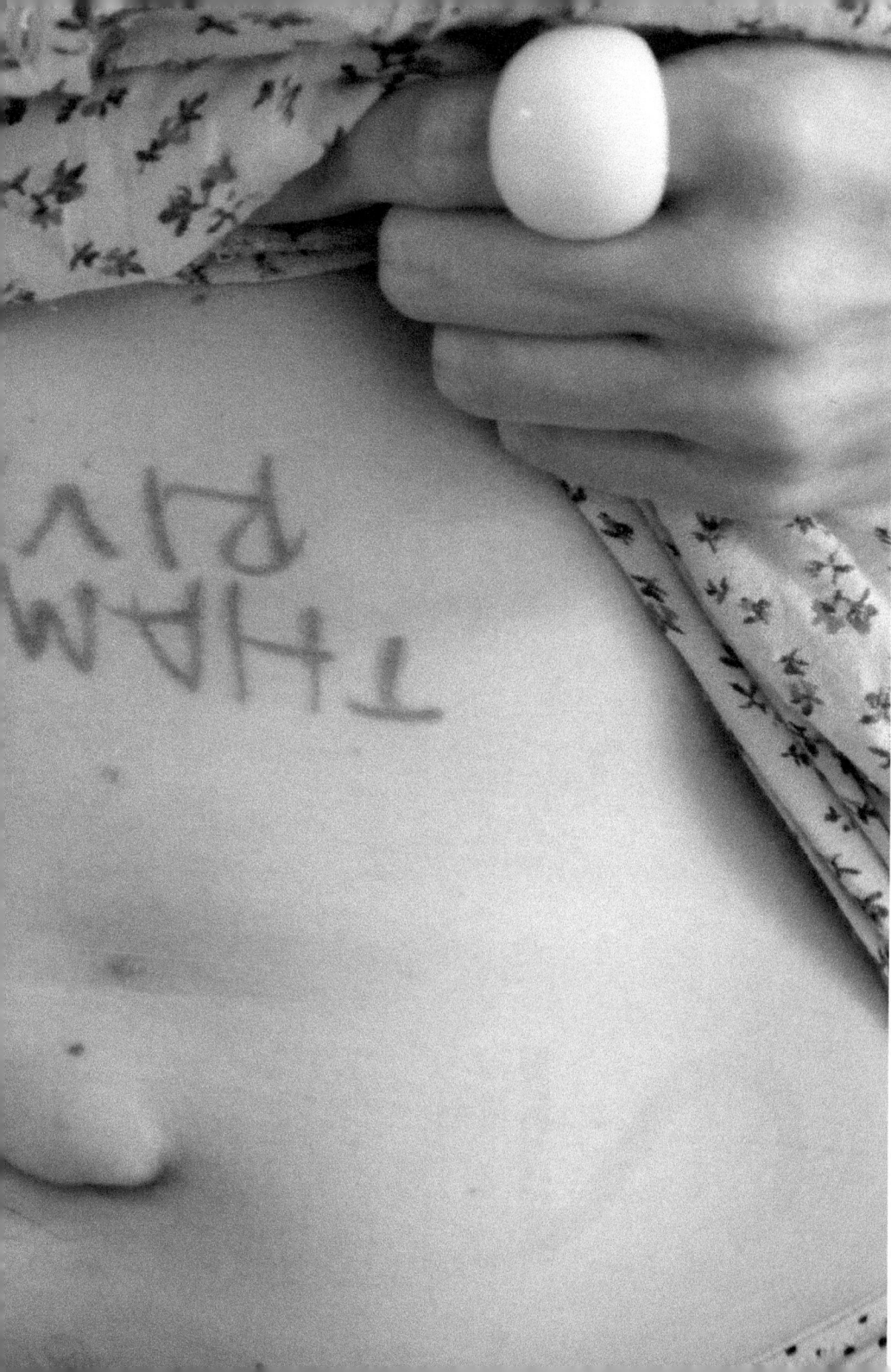

2

situat
edness

Re-situating Precarity in Times of Crisis: Interdepend- ence and Displacement across City-sites

by Manuela Zechner[1]

1   All references and links have last been accessed in June 2015.

#precarity   #situatedness   #mobility
#neoliberalism   #displacement   #inhabiting
#care

PART 1
(RE)SITUATING
OURSELVES
IN PRECARITY

Precarious (adj.): 1640s, a legal word, "held through the favor of another," from Latin precarius "obtained by asking or praying," from prex (genitive precis) "entreaty, prayer"[…]. Notion of "dependent on the will of another" led to extended sense "risky, dangerous, uncertain" (1680s). "No word is more unskillfully used than this with its derivatives. It is used for uncertain in all its senses; but it only means uncertain, as dependent on others"

Online Etymology Dictionary, 'Precarious'

A thing has as many meanings as there are forces capable of seizing it. Gilles Deleuze, Nietzsche and Philosophy

Precarity in (the) crisis

It looks like 'the crisis' – in its overlapping economic, social, institutional and environmental aspects – has brought the word 'precarity' back to its root. We can let go of some of the more uncomfortable autonomist affirmations of post-fordism and the liberties of the cognitariat and take our understanding and hoping about our precarious conditions elsewhere, to the sphere of social reproduction, of need, of care and networks of support. In the European peripheries shaken by economic crisis – the so-called PIIGS, or indeed even the eastern peripheries that are in permanent crisis – these shifts have been underway for a while.

The policies of neoliberal experimentation known as 'crisis' in Europe have meant such fast and wild welfare dismantling that to speak of precarity now is no longer the same as in 2004. Since 2008, poverty again came to be visible in the homes and streets of the European continent, particularly in the most affected peripheries, and in many places politics has thus come to be about needs as much as about desires. This has, though we witnessed it quite unwittingly, liberated us from the extolling politics of desire that grew with the various neoliberal bubbles in the 90s and early 2000s. Both in everyday economic life and in politics, the sky stopped being the limit, credit stopped promising quite so much, and everyday and material relations got a lot a more real and gritty. With this, precarity also could be returned to its etymological starting point: uncertainty and/in dependency on others.

Not just a vague sense of uncertainty, or a concrete malaise about exploitation and unemployment, but a sense of dependency. On one another, in society, in streets, in neighbourhoods. That was 2011. Dependency on one another also in homes, not only in the romantic sense of 'having to stick together' but also in the sense of rising domestic violence and women bearing the burden of austerity. The withdrawal of state support and the quick rise of unemployment means that with our everyday, our paradigm of life and survival changes. Moving from precarious employment – flexible, insecure, exploitative – to possibly no employment at all implies a deep shift. A new politics of social reproduction was born after 2013, with a strong sense of the importance of mutual support and care in the everyday. We started working on projects on Radical Collective Care[2], on Social Reproduction[3], tried to rethink the relation between need and desire[4].

A new set of problems and challenges came to be important, to do with ways of organising life in common: questions that precarity movements hadn't raised quite so directly and explicitly. In speaking about precarity, discussions shifted from work to life. From making a living to surviving. For many, unemployment and economic impasse became a hard reality; for many others, a very real and scary possibility. Our gaze as a precarious generation shifted, in those years after 2011. Emmigration, returning to live with the family[5], borrowing money – all those showed how much we needed others, emotionally, materially, socially.

The movements of the Juventud Sin Futuro ('Youth without a future', networks of Spanish Emmigrés abroad) and Marea Granate signalled that for many people of the so-called X and Y generations (born between the 80s and the 2000s), mobility isn't what it used to be. Not study abroad or Erasmus programmes, but the relatively choiceless decision to go elsewhere to make a living: migration. 'When the door shuts behind you, you know you are a migrant' (Precarity Office

83

2   The Radical Collective Care Practices Project
http://radicalcollectivecare.blogspot.com.es/
3   Manuela Zechner and Bue Hansen (2014), Social Reproduction and Collective Care, The Occupied Times of London
http://theoccupiedtimes.org/?p=14000
4   Social reproduction between need and desire: a reading group. Murmurae @ La Electrodoméstica, organised by Bue Hansen.
https://murmurae.wordpress.com/proyectos/social-reproduction-between-need-and-desire-reading-group/
5   See Shiv Malik (2014), The dependent generation: half young European adults live with their parents. The Guardian, march 2014.
http://www.theguardian.com/society/2014/mar/24/dependent-generation-half-young-european-adults-live-parents

Vienna).[6] We organised around that, around that transnational precarity and the need for new networks of care and solidarity that it called for. Tens of thousands of relatively young people abandoned the hardening outer crust of the European Butterbrot and told their own stories, made their own political claims, built their own networks.

So precarity stopped being all about employers, working conditions, contracts and laws and started to be more about the other we depend on. What and who to rely on once you've been swept from the doorsteps of what looked like a prospective middle class life, to a future of precarity? When the idea of a job or of a contract sounds like an abstraction, slightly unattainable? The processes of de-classing that economic crisis and austerity has meant in Europe are deep in terms of their subjective and social implications. Instead of asking what to go by, many of us also asked who and what to rely on in building a life. This latter question rang particularly relevant in the ears of generation X, those moving into their 30s and towards a phase in life where youth stops being the paradigm to go by. Maybe indeed youth would never have stopped being our paradigm, without this crisis – we might be working away on slogans for bullshit marketing and lifestyle industries still, sipping lattés and talking about the creative industries. What a nightmare.

This crisis was about ecology and collectivity as much as economy and finance, the world soon noted. In that sense, precarity came to be about an art of life in a new way: not as the fanciful art of lifestyle, but rather as an art of looking after life, caring for oneself and others, minding one's interdependency in as meaningful a way as possible. Art in the sense of learning, practice, skill, suitableness, preparation, manner/mode, fitting together (as indicated by etymology), as ongoing articulation with something at stake. If pre-crisis precarity was an optional way of viewing one's life, the new precarity appears as more of an inevitable reality: couched less in the lamenting of privileges that will be lost, rooted more strongly in a sense of interdependence and fragility.

84

situatedness

6   See the 2014-15 events of Precarity Office Vienna https://www.facebook.com/pages/Precarity-Office-Vienna/441185905996710

As this was happening, precarity ceased to be a buzzword or watchword – I say this from the viewpoint of the social movements I passed through in England, Austria and Spain particularly, but I'm pretty convinced that this dynamic affected many other places shaken by economic crisis too. In the Euro-Mediterranean, where Mayday movements initially took their start around 2004, the precarity discourse changed character quite soon after the economic crisis hit. In the European centre, where precarity organising emerged later, this shift took longer and is possibly still in process as I write in spring 2016. I write from between those European geographies here. Inspired scholars can do a discourse analysis to prove or disprove me here, for sure there is much to be said about the nuances of this shift or transformation of precarity in different texts and movements.

What I am pointing to here is the new cycles of experimentation – political as well as existential – that we've seen take off on the crusty old continent (and possibly beyond, but someone else needs to tell those stories). These stem from of displacement in the triple sense of mobile-migratory, class and professional shake-up. A lot of shifts in biographical and existential referents and vectors, accompanying shifts in the dominant mode of re/production and in geopolitics. Of course austerity didn't just happen, it is a way of restructuring this very social fabric and its imaginaries. A social fabric and imaginary building on post-war welfare states and social democracies, particularly in the centre/south of Europe. The social model of austerity seeks to drive down wages, fragment and divide society, increase competitivness, and it achieves all that. But it also produces counter-movements and counter-gestures, that we think differently about who we are in relation to others.

Goodbye middle class?
A brief (hi)story and cloudy horizon

We can speak about these developments in terms of de-classing, of a broad tendency of downward social mobility. Ups, we thought social mobility only went upward! Reading the fine print of the package insert, we can now see that's not the case. There was always also downward, and now the package itself is all about that.

Camille Peugny describes three interconnected levels of declassing, pointing to how these concretely play out in people's lives.

(1) Familial or intergenerational declassing (loss of status, unemployment)
(2) Personal or biographical declassing (uprooting)
(3) Educational or meritocratic declassing (devaluation of human capital)[7]

These imply saying goodbye to certain expectations: of having a pension, of having social security, working towards one's own house[8], of driving a (new) car, building a family or starting a business. The expectations that were shattered are the expectations of the middle class, expectations shared by that class as much as those below it: the middle class has been the telos of economy and society in Europe since after the great wars. Everybody had to go with it, even if that meant faking to be better or worse off than one really was.

The middle class and the welfare state are deeply linked in their beginnings and also in their contemporary decline in Europe. The middle class in Europe provided not just a strong base for markets and economies since the industrial revolution, but is also a pillar of democratic and subjective forms. The middle class had its big boost during the European post-war economic upturn in symbiosis with the welfare state: this strongly shaped the lives of the generations entering the labour market between the 1950's and the 80's. Those twenty years of glory, growth, near-full employment, rising wages, social security and baby booms were formative to the generation of my parents. They were the 'normal' (real or projected) that most Europeans grew into or grew up with in the latter half of the 20th century. But

7   Camille Peugny (2009), Le déclassement. Paris: Grasset.
8   See this article by Jenn Ashworth (2014), Generation rental. The Guardian, march 2014: http://www.theguardian.com/society/2014/mar/16/generation-rental-housing-crisis-shortage

already in the course of the 70's, neoliberalism's biopolitical paradigm began to transform economic and social systems, the lives of those who entered the labour market post-80s were increasingly shaped by falling wages, a shrinking public sector and welfare state, insecure contracts, the dismantling of pension schemes... the social contract of growth by welfare and consumption gave way to the neo-liberal one of growth by competitiveness and debt. By the 90s this started to mark a clear paradigm shift, and by 2010 it had run itself ad absurdum in financial and debt-related crisis. So here we are.

Those of us who grew up with post-war parents, the generation in pre-millennium EU accession countries, grew up to expect a middle class life. Middle class child-raising is notorious for its emphasis on education, civil citizenship and stability. Many of us pre-millennium kids had a great time studying, enabled by our parent's employment, public education and family support. By the time we graduated to enter the labour market, post-millennium, we however found a very different set of possibilities than those our parents had. Study, find a stable job, get a car, buy a house, have children, work until your pension kicks in, then have a calm last few decades at home or travelling: for most of us, this is no longer really in the cards.

For those in a precarious or working-class position, buying into the middle-class dream has largely meant accessing credit, and largely resulted in poverty. Poverty has risen quite starkly after 2008 in Europe[9], but the future is still being sold to people with scarce means: sub-primes and dodgy credit cards have not gone away. Mortgages are a key bubble dispositif for selling middle class life even when real wages make such life impossible (in the UK, over 60% of poor people have mortgages)[10]. The telos of middle class life has been shaking, but to be able to reject its promises,

9   In 2010, poverty (earning less than 60% of national median income) was between 17–20% in peripheral countries such as Portugal, Italy, Spain, Greece, Poland, Romania or the UK. See this study by Inequality Watch for example http://inequalitywatch.eu/ spip.php?article99
10   Julian Knight, First-time buyers on poverty 'knife edge', BBC News, august 2005. http://news.bbc.co.uk/2/hi/business/4081596.stm

there need to be other structures and resources to draw on for survival and self-valorization.

In this sense, struggles around housing and mortgages, such as the Spanish PAH[11], the London E15 mothers[12] or Kotti und Co[13], are not just key struggles around social reproduction, but also full-blown laboratories for de- and re-subjectivation. Forced to drop the same old catalogue of individualist consumer desires, people find collective strength in struggles and convivial experiments, building new common infrastructures. Powerful social struggles are always about becoming something else collectively and individually; in this case, it is middle class life they question and put in crisis. Their force in propelling broader social change lies in their ability to subvert the identification with middle-class values. They do this in a double movement: scandalizing the failure of middle-class security nets (bank loans, rising wages,...) is the superficial side thereof; powerful modes of collective organizing and composition, through mutual support, care and struggle are the deep end thereof. They transform the very subject of politics, not just the subject matter of claims.

Citizenship and cities sites
of struggle beyond the middle class

To think about the possible futures of these movements, it is useful to go a bit further back briefly, in the history of the middle class and citizenship. Indeed the growth of cities, as enabled by a new class of merchants growing between the peasants and the aristocracy, goes hand in hand with the growth of the bourgeoisie, leading into middle class urban populations. This class has been key to forming our contemporary images of citizenship, of what a 'normal' citizen is supposed to be and what rights and responsibilities (s)he

11   See for example this introduction to the PAH which I wrote for the Radical Collective Care Practices blog.
http://radicalcollectivecare.blogspot.com.es/2013/08/the-plataforma-de-afectados-por-la.html
12   The Focus E15 campaign http://focuse15.org/
13   In Germany, the Kotti und Co struggle is a vital one.
http://kottiundco.net/english/ as well as the popular legislative campaign for rent controls https://mietenvolksentscheidberlin.de/

is supposed to have (needless to say, the model was the white male professional). It is the subversion of this model that is at stake in working towards a post-middle-class horizon, towards other ways of thinking belonging and inhabiting.

Cities are key sites for the negotiation of belonging and inhabiting. They matter a lot more to most people in my generation than do nations, particularly to those of us who feel we belong to several places at once. Many people's modes of inhabiting European cities have changed in recent years: neighbourhood organizing has become possible again; squares, streets, public spaces and institutions have been occupied and reshaped; movements for urban commons and food production intensified; powerful new municipal movements have emerged to reclaim the city as space for democracy and commons.[14] The downtrodden middle class plays a significant role in driving this, channeling their anger into new platforms of struggle.

These struggles will likely last as long as there is an existential horizon of insecurity and loneliness, and a need to find one another. At the institutional level, they will almost certainly produce a new political class that eventually will content itself with the security it created (hopefully not just for itself but also for others). Already now, in 2016, notions of having overcome crisis and reached economic growth again are quite familiar, and certainly these will keep returning in different cycles of the years and decades to come. If the assumption that capitalism will inevitably undo itself in its current form, sooner or later, is correct, then these ups and downs will only be temporary however. The key question will still be that of social reproduction, and of undoing the middle class telos. One key vector of these struggles to come is care.

Goodbye liberal autonomous subject

Across many struggles, a new ethics of care has emerged to address interdependence from a viewpoint beyond the welfare state, starting debates and instituting infrastructures

14   Barcelona en Comú: the city as horizon for radical democracy.
A text I wrote for Roarmag in early 2015 http://roarmag.org/2015/03/
barcelona-en-comu-guanyem/

of social care. Solidarity clinics and kitchens in Greece, Spanish movements revindicating care work and feminist economics[15], translocal movements of solidarity economy and transition, cooperativist movements, housing struggles, campaigns against fracking and waste dumping, refugee solidarity movements have kept European elites on their feet in recent years. The political subject these struggles depart from is in fact one of interdependence and of care, not the male autonomous one.

If, as the etymological interpretation at the beginning of this text claims, 'precarious' particularly means 'uncertain' in the sense of being 'dependent on others' – dependent on asking, begging, praying – then it points to a subject beyond the liberal notions of autonomy and freedom. The gesture of asking, of addressing the other with a request, defies the very subjectivities upon which our Western societies have been built, whereby every 'man' tends to his own business and fends on his own, managing his own resources and opportunities, claiming his very individual rights.

While being dependent on others may indeed have been the norm for most people at most times, necessitating respectful and caring relations that allow for reciprocity and support, liberalism has us believe that independence is the norm. Neoliberalism then takes this to another level of atomization, turning every soul into a little business, closing every body in on itself. At the same time, those privileged enough can universalize themselves, consider their individual position as universal. When it becomes clear that independence and liberal universalism are a symptom of privilege and geopolitical and cultural isolation, new possible starting points for subjectivity and struggle emerge.

Montserrat Galceran recently reported that indigenous women in Ecuador, when asked about what model of state and forms of rights they want, said they didn't want to be independent, that they were happy being dependent. What they want is a buena vida, a good life, rather than an estado de bienestar, a welfare state. Interdependence

15   For instance the Fira de Economia Feminista in Barcelona, a gathering of grassroots feminist movements and thinkers https://firaeconomiafeminista.wordpress.com/

as a dignified way of life that respects nature and its resources, that can do without the fabrication of illusions of autonomy via the state or market, but rather demands to depend on others in well-becoming ways.

When did it ever occur to us that dependence on others could be the most rich and dignified way of existing? And, if we go with that general idea, what criteria and compasses do we need in order to invent ways of navigating interdependency in our first-world contexts? Our indigenousness has been sucked out of us hundreds of years ago in Europe, little is left of an intimate relation to the land (beyond spooky nationalisms); our families are in tatters, little tempts us to return them to their original (patriarchal and/or nuclear) ways. So where can we start from in affirming and sustaining interdependency?

Here is where precarity can be one possible point of return. If we take a bastard etymological approach to the word 'precarity', or indeed more of a phonetic one, we may say 'pre'-'care'-'ity'. In fact precarity is a state of pre-care: the precarious are those not quite in a position to care and support in a sustained way, those who have to keep holding out their hand, unstable and insecure enough never to know they'll have enough to pass it around. Precarity, as a proletarianized form of interdependency, is also about being unable to give, to host and offer to others.

And yet the precarious are ever-exploited, ever giving and offering themselves to the labour market, pushed into badly paid jobs, in a sort of transcendentally infantilizing dynamic. With the crisis, the aspiration to make it to that stable place from which one can give (which perhaps most poignantly crystallizes in our inability to sustain another life, be it to have children or to care for our elders, because we have too little money, too little security, too unstable a schedule, too scattered a life) comes to center somewhat less on the wage and increasingly also on self-organized support structures and ways of working.

So the questions we must ask with a post-middle-class horizon in mind concern ecologies of inhabitation, networks of care and economies of the commons. Not as a fashion or religion, not as a new telos, but as lived and felt questions and practices to always return to. As places to draw strength from and breath towards, with every blow of failure, disappointment or repression. Because these horizons are not achieved in quick struggle, they are not built in speedy experiments, they are assembled bit by bit and constantly subject to reframing, dismantling, rebuilding. We will not have our new societies, our new institutions and our new subjectivities in a flash: because they don't yet exist, nor does a perfect plan for them exist. They hinge on our attention and care at every moment, in tune with our bodies and their capacities.

How do we want to enter into a position where we can care, where we can give to those around us? How can we care without slipping into subaltern roles (housewives) or power games (fatherly or motherly control)? Precarity infantilizes us when we have no tools to develop collective support: it turns us into children who merely depend, without being able to give. I think/feel that this problem affects us as a generation. We struggle to get to the 'care' part because of precarity, then we either take the nuclear family route to care, or often remain somewhat lonely. Our liberal rights and liberties are of little help in the face of this problem. This is a challenge that requires us to situate ourselves: to face the current moment of class displacement (and all the other facets of displacement too) with subjective and collective intelligence. How might we situate ourselves within a paradigm of interdependency, against and within the displacement that shapes our lives today?

PART 2
SITUATING OURSELVES
IN DISPLACEMENT

What does is mean to struggle against precarity, globalization and neoliberalism in embodied terms? How do we forge networks of care, post-national struggles and solidarities in our everyday? When do we resist displacement and how do we resist through displacement? How do we think consistency and sustainability? What terms serve us to think an ethics and politics of displacement

– situated/adrift, local/global, intimate/alienated, individual/collective, independent/interdependent, coming/going, flight/promise, transversality/intersectionality? What are the ways in which contemporary practices of displacement are produced by the neoliberal paradigm and embedded within structures and systems of governance?[16]

Where is home?

For precarity to give way to care and sustainable forms of everyday reproduction, other kinds of pacts and relationships must become possible. And so we must re-imagine not just other relationships but also other territories; to situate the where of our relations, the common frameworks and reference points, common routes and places of dwelling.
To be less essentialist and more pragmatic about our coexisting and co-belonging. Without territorial and habitual reference points, we are left to anxiety, cutting us off from the world around us. Reference points can mean shared places and routines as well as common notions and practices, shared histories and narratives.[17] In times of displacement, of itinerancy and passing through, the challenge is to find such new referents together with others.
Displacement and disorientation, as key neoliberal dynamics, operate across many scales, from intimate relations

16   Opening questions of the 'Situating oneself in displacement' autumn lab at La Electrodoméstica in Barcelona, October 2014. Written by myself and Paula Cobo-Guevara. https://laelectrodomestica.wordpress.com/2014/07/21/situating-oneself-autumn-laboratory/
17   A recent study found that tattoo culture has boomed in the past ten years, particularly with young US millennials (people born between 80s-2000s), a majority of which has tattoos apparently). The study concludes that tattoos function as 'anchors' within which people inscribe their memories and experiences, stabilizing a sense of identity in a world that rapidly changes and offers them little stability. James Cook's sailors began to keep tattoo souvenirs from their journeys through the south pacific in the 1700s, reminders of beautiful encounters but also spiritual anchors for precarious ventures far from home that often came close to death. Anchors, reference points, signposts, reminders: they calm our anxiety, that sense of being adrift and lost in a world that moves too fast or wildly (anxiety, unlike fear, has no clear object). Gilbert Simondon describes anxiety as the loss of points of reference, which can lead to a disintegration of the subject (Simondon, L'individuation).

to housing and migration. Without wanting to conflate different experiences here, I will work though 'displacement' as broad concept to touch on some concrete instances. How to inhabit and dwell, if we can't find ways of relating, of knowing and trusting? How do we end up embodying displacement? A friend recently posted this on Facebook:

> "Where do you fly in from?" the lady at the airport asks me. It takes me a few seconds to remember and utter the name of the nth connect flight airport I flew from over the last few days. But her next question gets me even further off guard "Where do you live?" she says dryly with her schooled rigor and suspicion. I look into her eyes, embarrassed, I don't even know where I am, and having lived in 7 countries over the last 5 years doesn't help me too much. And then the saving word "Here. I live here!"[18]

These are not the words of a jet-setting businesswoman, but of a young researcher from Eastern Europe, subject to the laws of academic 'mobility', struggling to find stable employment at any university, compelled to follow a chain of grants and short-term contracts in different places.

The airport is where precarity, displacement and individualization often meet. A friend from London, an Italian migrant academic in her early 30s, points out how this conjunction relates to time horizons:

> [...] all of us were quite individualized, all of us in the group of friends in London, because we weren't committed to anything long term; we didn't have family responsibility, we didn't have older people to care for, we were quite a good prototype of the neoliberal self-entrepreneurial individual: critical and self-reflexive but absolutely free to reinvent ourselves all the time, without commitment, responsibility. And so the fragility of this is more than the

18   Mariya on Facebook, winter 2014.

fragility of a more traditional way of owing
to each other and being part of the same family,
of having social duties almost because of
your role, because of your family position. But
at the same time, there were commitments
and we did create other forms of expectations
between colleagues, between friends, between people sharing political projects maybe.
But it is still a kind of commitment that will
always forgive…
the fact that at some time you will go. It is
your choice, you're always free to leave eventually, and actually maybe people would envy
you if you manage.[19]

And so precarity leaves us fending for ourselves, even if we
wish to stay loyal and put. In the end our decisions will
only be made in relation to ourselves, at most with a partner
and only rarely with children attached. This may be seen
to be even lonelier than the nuclear family, or indeed preferable
to the nuclear family as it opens to other modes of thinking
co-responsibility and care. Precarity, as well as the demise
of the middle class, is an ambivalent phenomena; problematic
but also opening onto new possibilities.[20]
  This has led many of us to think about commitment, inhabitation and situatedness beyond both the nuclear family
and the opportunistic network: neither the individualization of
a small normative reproductive units folded in on themselves nor the hyper-connected individualization of networking
and entrepreneurial competition. In the 'old' paradigm of
precarity, this was a moral standpoint and lifestyle choice: now
it's more of an everyday question, banal and inevitable in
its requiring a solution. In my experience, this mostly means
working through different experimental constellations of

19   Interview with Gabriella, London 2012. Taken from my Phd thesis,
'The world we desire is one we create and care for together'.
Queen Mary University London, 2013, not yet published.
20   I talk about that here: Precariousness beyond creativity: some
inflexions on care and collectivity, in: Maps of Precariousness,
edited by E. Armano, A. Murgia. Bologna, Odoya, 2012. http://de.
scribd.com/doc/218594343/Mappe-della-precarieta-Volume-2-pdf

commitment; trying and failing with building sustainable relations and commons.

Precarious care networks
in the city

The city is a key site in this respect. Not just because more and more people keep moving to cities, but because the question of post-welfare precarity within which I am situating this text is a very urban one. Our networks of everyday life, care and support are mostly within cities; our trajectories run between cities. Our cities grow (mostly). What, then, is the meaning of the constitutive parts of the city for the creation of commons and support/care?

A quick anatomy of city immediately yields terms like neighbourhood, district, transport lines, zones, outskirts, centre, rent, speculation, distance, population. We can dive even in deeper to get to streets, spaces, homes, institutions, histories, languages, dialects, identities, struggles. And if we think of our everyday networks, we can get to flatshares, dinners, parties, public events, parks, cafés, occasionally streets, but also to Skypes, time zones, instant messages (Whatsapp and the like), everyday snapshots or selfies of friends and family, homes in other cities. The recent golden age of displacement has meant many circuits of care are geographically dispersed, from friends (the old ones from 'home', the ones from studying, the ones from here and there, the current ones) to family (the ones at 'home', the ones who moved). It can be interesting and useful to make maps of displacement relating to generations of family and friends, and maps of our care networks in the city and across cities. [21]

21   I've been developing techniques of care network mapping for a while, for instance in the Nanopolitics Handbook where you can find a text about militant families and an instruction for mapping exercise. Recently, in a course on 'The city, Care and Infrastructures of the Commons' we adapted those to specific urban territories, mapping forms of interdependency and sharing resources at an individual as well as collective level. Such experiments can be quite useful for visualizing and analyzing the singular and recurrent configurations and problems of care networks in the city, and across cities. See here for the Nanopolitics Handbook http://www.minorcompositions.info/?p=590#more-590 and here for the Care/Commons/City course: http://nocionescomunesbcn.net/2014/11/15/curso-como-cono-se-sostiene-esto/

At a broader level, the city is itself a product of displacement and has many processes of displacement occuring internally. It is important to have those in mind when situating oneself in (trans)urban territories, since displacement is one of the major incisions in systems of reproduction and networks of care. People who leave may be replaceable by others in certain functions relating to the commons; the closer we come to care however, the more singular the relations and the less possible it is to substitute one person with another (one of the key points in discussions about care work). When people move from close constellations of support, especially when there is strong interdependency (material and/or emotional), they remain referents. We can see this in care chains (when mothers migrate to work as care-givers abroad for instance) as well as in what we might call 'chains or networks of mobility'.

As those who move, our relation to such reconfigurations of care systems tends to be deeply ambivalent. It always comes with letting people down. It's hard and sometimes impossible to make this a collective process – displacement individualizes. Our entanglement with processes of capitalist extraction and urbanization is something we bitterly feel as mobile/migratory subjects. The search for sustainable forms of life and community can be full of contradictions, particularly in neoliberalism.

In what follows, and to conclude, I will briefly think through three topologies causing dispacement within the of city that effect our ways of inhabiting together: travel, gentrification and urbanization. These all come with specific affects: loneliness, guilt, escapism, melancholy, anxiety.

Travel / the city as lonely island. Sometimes we pass through the city without touching base with anyone, inhabit our own cities like passengers or consumers. We can do that even if our stay there is long – the figure of the expat comes to mind – not speaking to neighbors or friends, sticking to the internet. Sometimes it's easier to inhabit the virtual space and relations of the internet than to land where our bodies are at. The bigger a city, the more it offers itself for drifting through as if it were a deserted an island, making no contact with people beyond the exchange of money or rudimentary information, becoming itself a kind of virtual, abstract space.

Urbanization / the city as telos. The city, even though imperceptible to many a traveler's eye, is also marked by displacement from the rural to the urban. Besides the jumping and jet-setting between cities, there is a steady inflow or rural bodies that arrive to make up the underclass, notably at the margins of cities (suburbs, peripheral zones, slums, banlieues, favelas, worker settlements). Displacement from the rural to the urban, from non-industrialized to industrialized (for there is no city without industry, and no industry without urbanization) has a long and partially exhausted history in Europe, but it still marks the geographies of the city. How to interact with this telos of the city, and the peripheries it draws from (and produces)? This is an important question if we are to step outside the horizon of the urban middle class and build new solidarities.

John Bellamy Foster points out[22] that the conflict between the city and country can be seen as equally powerful as the one between labour and capital (the latter being internal to the city). The city is a result of violence: a good part of the people moving from the country to the city do so because they are forcefully displaced and can see no future there in terms of employment or social life. Between 62-84% of world poverty is rural (in Europe, 62,8% of poverty is rural and 37,2% urban)[23]. Cities are growing at vertiginous speed. Abandoning them in an act of voluntarism is not an option for most people, yet it remains interesting to contemplate the possibility of weaving new continuities across the rural and metropolitan. Many new and old practices of co-inhabiting, economy and production point this way: squatting land, local agricultural coops, agroecological networks, shared convivial spaces in the countryside, reviving depopulated villages as experimental micro-municipalities, etc.[24].

22   John Bellamy Foster (2013) Marx and the Rift in the universal metabolism of nature. Monthly Review, Dec 2013 http://monthly review.org/2013/12/01/marx-rift-universal-metabolism-nature/
23   See these statistics from 2014 for instance http://www.ophi.org. uk/wp-content/uploads/Poverty-in-Rural-and-Urban-Areas-Direct-Comparisons-using-the-Global-MPI-2014.pdf?0a8fd7
24   Including not just organic food coops and agroecological networks (the Italian rete GAS or Genuino Clandestino networks for instance), but also rural squatting and collective experiments in buying old rural spaces for open use (eg. Mühle Nikitsch/AT, Performing Arts Forum Reims/FR).

Gentrification / the city as marked by property. This leads us to one of the most intense internal displacement processes in neoliberal cities, emerging with the financialization of spaces, habitats and infrastructures as 'assets' open for trading and speculation. Rising rents and property prices, construction sites, new condos and empty flats, fancy neighborhoods, organic food, cupcakes; these all seem to revolve around the middle class as agent of acquisition and conquest. Cities may indeed, to some extent, be playgrounds for the upper middle classes, but for most the playground is inaccessible spectacle: for you need capital to speculate, and subaltern and precarious city dwellers have no access to credit, not even to the world of sub-primes, for lack of legal or stable work.

The affects in this dynamic are guilt, anxiety, depression and anger, for most precarious dwellers. For gentrification begins with precarious trendiness and goes via the upwardly mobile to the upper middle and then shamelessly rich classes. From migrant or working class communities to squatters and bohemians, to the cultural folk, to the yummy mummies and young professionals, etc... What to do about being cannon fodder of capitalist accumulation and investment?

It's hard to combat this massive redistribution of wealth when there is no local resilience; speculation and fast-transit inhabitation make them very hard to build. Still only common struggles can channel the disempowerment,... sad affects into anger, rage and solidarity. We wrote about this in relation to London, in the Nanopolitics Handbook[25], and experimented with ways of collectively inhabiting our fast-changing neighborhoods. We also began to wonder about what we project into cities and what keeps us there – from 'making it' career-wise, to being in a certain scene or circuit, to being close to certain people or places, or having certain kinds of safety and resource.

25   See Nanopolitics Group (2013) Un/making sense, moving together: nanopolitical experimentes in the neoliberal city. In: Nanopolitics Handbook, pp.19 – 39. http://www.minorcompositions. info/?p=590#more-590

99

Figures of Fragility in Displacement: Situating Ourselves in Displacement

by (some) Grupo Esquizo[1]

1   Nizaiá Cassián, Raquel Sánchez, Miriam Sol, Lucía Serra.
Text translated from Castellano by Paula Cobo-Guevara

* Parts of this text correspond to some working notes and a loose transcription from a schizo Barcelona-session carried out at the Laboratory. The notes and exercises are placed in chronological order. Each block will be headed by a short text describing the subject matter that we addressed in each of the exercises. This text is divided into three parts
Alice, La Güera, La Puente.

PART 1
ALICE.
'BEING SO MANY
SIZES IN A DAY IS VERY
CONFUSING'

We are constantly moving between contexts, cities, jobs, collectives, relations. And every time we arrive into a new place or situation we are faced – implicitly or explicitly – with all these questions: who are you, what do you do, where do you come from; from which country, but also from which discipline, from which collective or political trajectory?

In this session we would like to work around fragility in displacement. The fragility involved in being constantly flexible, adapting, with the feeling of waves and earthquakes under our feet. What kind of narratives can we experiment with to turn this individualized fragility into a collective matter? A matter of concern and a matter of care.

We like the word 'matter' because it addresses both a concern, an issue, something to be problematized. But not only as a rational, logocentric or discursive thing. It is not enough to think or reflect around it. Fragility as a matter of concern and a matter of care means to give account of the material and embodied conditions in which we experiment it and th wisdom, strategies and jury rigs we create to deal with this fragility in our networks and collectives.

We want to propose here a question as the starting point of this matter of concern and care: Who are you? What are you?

This is a question that is actually quite present in our everyday life. Not in a transcendent or existential way, but as a very concrete and embodied demand. Those who are in movement – in between, abroad, coming and going – are always in the need to introduce themselves. We think that we can all relate to this experience in some way.

Let's read a fragment from Alice in Wonderland addressing this question:

> The Caterpillar and Alice looked at each other for some time in silence: at last the Caterpillar took the hookah out of its mouth, and the Caterpillar. This was not an encouraging opening for a conversation. Alice replied, rather shyly, 'I--I hardly know, sir, just at present-- at least I know who I WAS when I got up this morning, but I think I must have been changed several times since then.' 'What do you mean by that?' said the Caterpillar sternly. 'Explain yourself!' 'I can't explain MYSELF, I'm afraid, sir' said Alice, 'because I'm not myself, you see.' 'I don't see,' said the Caterpillar. 'I'm afraid I can't put it more clearly,' Alice replied very politely, 'for I can't understand it myself to begin with; and being so many different sizes in a day is very confusing.' 'It isn't,' said the Caterpillar. 'Well, perhaps you haven't found it so yet,' said Alice; 'but when you have to turn into a chrysalis – you will some day, you know – and then after that into a butterfly, I should think you'll feel it a little queer, won't you?' 'Not a bit,' said the Caterpillar. 'Well, perhaps your feelings may be different,' said Alice; 'all I know is, it would feel very queer to ME.' 'You!' said the Caterpillar contemptuously. 'Who are YOU?' Which brought them back again to the beginning of the conversation.

What we get from this passage is that 'who we are' is a quite authoritarian and violent demand. There's certainty an ambiguity within this question; let's look at it in a two fold way: A mode of subjection, or normalization; those who are outside the norm or the normal are in a constant demand of identification and explanation of who they are. Here we would talk about identity and the construction of subject categories that actually subject. A disciplinary dispositive of normalization and individualization. What Foucault calls the confessionary dispositive brought into psychiatry but also into penal practices and many other social and institutional environments.

However, there's another side to this twofold experience. There is a powerful and strong gesture in the affirmation of who are. Civil rights movements have taken this strength as a place of dignity: Chicano, black, queer movements. The affirmation of who we are becomes a performative, strategic and productive gesture, which defends and builds the rights and territories of existence of this singularity.

Saying who we are, sometimes provides us the feeling of belonging to a certain territory or community. It helps us situate ourselves: I am a feminist. It is also a performative strategy of reappropriation and contestation: Soy bollera (I'm a dike). But we have the impression that quite often, one ends up with the feeling that these enunciative categories per se are quite limited. Not only limited to 'tell the truth of who we are', but limited in actually building the territories where we can be, and be with others. Saying 'I'm a feminist' doesn't build the conditions of possibility for new distributions of reproductive labour, for example. How then, do we give account of this embodiments and practices that constitute our everyday singularities and their territories?

Throughout this session we would like to work around this issues: identity, singularity, positionality. We are 'so many sizes in just one day' that we end up not knowing who and with whom we are. How do we give account of the trajectories that constitute the multiplicity of those many that we are? How do we deal in our collectives with the fragility of being constantly in the move, being so many sizes? How do we deal with the fragility of certain marks on our bodies?

We would like to work now with some figures of fragility in displacement. The figure we propose here is "La Güera." In this tension between who we are and where we belong to, we think some narratives from Chicana feminism can be quite inspiring. We will be working with the text 'La Güera' and some poems through out the session. La Güera is a text by Cherrie Moraga, a Chicana feminist that together with Gloria Anzaldua, published in 1981 a compilation called This bridge called my back. Writings by radical women of color.

Reading together
La Güera, part 1.

[mestiza, border, the non purity of our flesh, bodies in displacement]

(1)
(2)
(3)

(4)

Take a moment to read the first two pages of the text 'La Güera'.
Underline particular phrases that call your attention or that some how resound for you.
Choose a couple of sentences or words that evoke transit, shift, turn or displacement. How are trajectories, singularities, positionalities marked on the body?
We'll take now a few minutes to share our impressions in groups of 3 – 4.

Here we share a few paragraphs we discussed in groups.

'I am the very well educated daughter of a woman who, by the standards of this country, would be considered largely illiterate. My mother was born in Santa Paula, Southern California [...] she was the only daughter of six to marry an Anglo, my father. I remember all of my mother's stories, probably much better than she realizes. She is a fine storyteller,

104

situatedness

recalling every event of her life with the vivid-
ness of the present [...]

I was educated, and wore it with a keen sense
of pride and satisfaction, my head propped
up with the knowledge, from my mother, that
my life would be easier than hers. I was
educated; but more than this, I was "la güera":
fair-skinned. Born with the features of my
Chicana mother, but with the skin of my Anglo
father, I had it made. No one ever quite told
me this (that light was right), but I knew that
being light was something valued in my family
(who where all Chicano with the exception
of my father).

I experience, daily, a huge disparity between
what I was born into and what I was to grow up
to become. Because, (as Goldman suggest)
these stories my mother told me crept under
my "güera" skin. I had no choice but to enter
into the life of my mother, had no choice. I took
her life into my heart, but managed to keep
a lid on it as long as I feigned being the happy,
upwardly mobile heterosexual.

It wasn't until I acknowledge and confronted
my own lesbianism in the flesh, that my
heartfelt identification with and empathy for
my mothers oppression – due to being
poor, uneducated, and Chicana – was realized.
My lesbianism is the avenue through which
I have learned the most about silence
and oppression, and it continues to be the
most tactile reminder to me that we are
not free human beings.

    With this first part of the text we wanted to start with a few
basic ideas. Who we are is not a matter of purity, neither
is it something static. Who we are is not a matter of will or

voluntarism. We are inhabited by our life trajectories, by the marks on our bodies. We don't 'decide' who we are in a logocentric sense, but we enact it and embody it through flesh and practices.

Body Map – Who are you?
Exercise
[body marks, traces, categories embodied on our flesh]

How are all the singularities or labels that define ourselves, embodied in different parts of our flesh? Where on our bodies do we inhabit the terms, identities and positionalities by which we are (self) defined, named by others or inter-polated by the context? To work around these questions, we are going to make a cartography of a collective body.

(1) Instructions:
Let's sit down in a circle on the floor.
(2) Bring a pen and a notebook.
We'll make a short list of the terms that you have used to refer, identify, present or situate yourself. They might be terms related to your present life or some others that were very present in the past. Think also about those labels or categories that have been used by others regarding you, to name you or by which you've been identified:

a There can be general categories regarding age, gender, the place where you come from, sexual preference, i.e. lesbian, gay, hetero, european, latin, young, woman, a nickname regarding your physical appearance – like 'la güera'

b Regarding kinship and affective relations, ie: grandmother, son, partner

c Related to your profession or the work that you perform

d Terms in relation to the collectivities and/or communities to which you belong.

(3) Write them all down and pick out those five that seem the most significative: the ones that particularly resound in you or that have marked you the most. There might be those that cause you some kind of tension, terms you have already problematized in your life, or those that give you joy and a sense of belonging.

(4) Write each one of them on a post-it. If you had to point out one part of your body where each one of this five terms inhabits or is incarnated the most, where would it be? Take a couple of minutes to locate them, where do these terms reveal or disclose them selves more intensely on your flesh? Place the post-it on that part of your body or write it down directly on your skin.

(5) Let's walk around the room and take a moment to look at each other's marks.

(6) Now we are going to go from this embodied categories placed on our individual bodies, to transfer them on to a collective dimension, or collective body.

(7) Lets take some white tape to trace a silhouette of a body on the floor. Together we have to decide the characteristics we want to give to this outline: its size, shapes and volumes.

(8) Now, by pairs take out the labels that are right now covering your body and place them on the collective silhouette on the floor.

(9) Let us take some time to observe the different labels placed on the body and we'll take 10 minutes to share some thoughts about them.

"La Güera that is
not that blond"

We will continue with these figures of fragility in displacement. The figure we propose now is 'La Güera that is not that blond'. Cherrie Moraga talks about 'click' situations that put into question the stability or 'purity' of our embodied positionalities. We would like to continue with another fragment from the text. It will help us think how in certain moments of our lives and trajectories, this categories, labels, 'identities' or subjective enunciations become unstable. Destabilized. Take a moment to read pages 4–5 from the text 'La Güera'. We have taken a few fragments from the text that maybe can inspire us to think about our clicks.

> At the age of twenty-seven, it is frightening to acknowledge that I have internalized a racism and classism, where the object of oppression is not only someone outside of my skin but the someone inside my skin. In fact, to a large degree, the real battle with such oppression, for all of us, begins under the skin. I have had to confront the fact that much of what I value about being Chicana, about my family, has been subverted by anglo culture and my own cooperation with it. This realization did not occur to me overnight. For example, it wasn't until long after my graduation from the private college I'd attended in Los Angeles that I realized the major reason for my total alienation from and fear of my classmates was rooted in class and culture. CLICK.
>
> Three years after graduation, in an apple-orchard in Sonoma, a friend of mine (who comes from an Italian Irish working-class family) says to me, "Cherrie, no wonder you felt like such a nut in school. Most of the people there were white and rich." It was true. All along I had felt the difference, but not until I had put the words "class" and "color" to the experience, did my feelings make any sense. For years, I had berated myself for not being as "free" as my classmates. I completely bought that they simply had more guts than I did – to

rebel against their parents and run around the country hitchhiking, reading books and studying "art" [...] But I knew nothing about "privilege" then. White was right. Period. I could pass. If I got educated enough, there would never be any telling.

Three years after that, another CLICK. In a letter to Barbara Smith, I wrote:

I went to a concert where Ntosake Shange was reading. There, everything exploded for me. She was speaking a language that I knew – in the deepest parts of me – existed, and that I had ignored in my own feminist studies and even in my own writing. What Ntosake caught in me is the realization that in my development as a poet, I have, in many ways, denied the voice of my brown mother – the brown in me. [...]

The reading was agitating. Made me uncomfortable [...] I felt that I had to start all over again. That I turned only to the perceptions of white middle-class women to speak for me and all women. I am shocked by my own ignorance.

Sitting in that auditorium chair was the first time I had realized to the core of me that for years I had disowned the language I knew best – ignored the words and rhythms that were the closest to me. The sounds of my mother and aunts gossiping – half in English, half in Spanish – while drinking cerveza in the kitchen. And the hands – I had cut off the hands in my poems. But not in conversation; still the hands could not be kept down. Still they insisted on moving.

'A 'click turn'
Exercise

['click' turn, tactile reminder, trajectories,
stability – trajectory]

We will take a few minutes to think about a situation where
we've lived a kind of 'click' turn like the ones Moraga talks
about. An experience or a moment when something happened
to us that destabilized, confronted or put into question
our position, identity or the ground where we were standing
regarding the terms we identified in the first part.

Instructions:

(1)
(2) Think about a 'click situation'.
Identify what was you avenue or tactile
reminder. What was that affect/effect in which
that click took placed as an embodied
displacement?
(3)
Write one or two short sentences to give
account of that experience.
(4)
If anybody wants to share, we can take a
moment to read some of the experiences and
we will situate this click turns on the
collective body.

PART 3
LA PUENTE.

With this exercise we have thought about very singular or
somehow individual experiences. What we want to explore
now is in which spaces are we having the possibility to talk, to
share and to experiment with this clicks. Are we breaking
through this problem collectively or are we taking care of it,
individually? We would like again to start with a poem that
talks about another figure of fragility.

We are constantly translating, building and sustaining
bridges, filling the gaps between those many that we are.

This bridge
called my back

I've had enough
I'm sick of seeing and touching
Both sides of things
Sick of being the damn bridge
for everybody

Nobody
Can talk to anybody
Without me Right?
I explain my mother to my father my father
to my little sister
My little sister to my brother my brother to
the white feminists
The white feminists to the Black church
folks the Black church folks
To the Ex-hippies the ex-hippies to the
Black separatists the
Black separatists to the artists the artists
to my friends' parents...
Then
I've got the explain myself
To everybody
I do more translating
Than the Gawdamn U.N.
Forget it
I'm sick of it
I'm sick of filling in your gaps
Sick of being your insurance against
The isolation of your self-imposed
limitations
Sick of being the crazy
at your holiday dinners

Sick of being the odd one
at your Sunday Brunches
Sick of being the sole Black friend
to 34 individual white people

Find another connection
to the rest of the world
Find something else to make you legitimate
Find some other way to be political and hip
I will not be the bridge to your womanhood
Your manhood
Your human-ness
I'm sick of reminding you not to
Close off too tight for too long
I'm sick of mediating with your worst self
On behalf you your better selves

I am sick
Of having to remind you
To breathe
Before you suffocate
Your own fool self
Forget it
Stretch or drown
Evolve or die
The bridge I must be
Is the bridge to my own power
I must translate
My own fears
Mediate
My own weaknesses
I must be the bridge to nowhere
But my true self
And then
I will be useful

Donna Kate Rush

111

'La puente'
Exercise

Let's look at the map that we have made on our collective
body. Do you feel related in anyway to those other categories that are not yours? Think on specific gestures that enable
you to link different positionalities? Which spaces vincuhu-
late or link this positionalities; which of these links (or 'bridges')
are weak or do not exist? In which spaces are you able
to develop a territory for sharing, inhabit, etc? How are you
effected by ie: being a feminist at the University, how does being a militant affect within your family? How do you deal
with being a tom-boy/lesbian ('bollera') at your work? How do
you deal with being middle/upper class in your militancy/
activism? How do you deal with being a male within a your
female partners in the context of a political collectivity?

Let's visualize the 'puentes' (links) between these spaces in a very superficial way…

Notes and reflections:

We have tried to map which are the spaces in which we feel interpolated, challenged; which are those scratches in our bodies. This first part of the exercise allowed us to map those spaces in which we feel fixed?; also map our spaces of potency and subjection towards our identities and positionalities? Let's identify those positionalities, those subjectivities; they are immanently related to those physical and symbolical spaces that we inhabit; and go through some questions together: ↙ What are the most common scratches of our bodies?   → Which are the relationships that constitute us?   ↓ To what spaces do we set,

settle?   ↗ What are those posi-
tions/positionalities in which we
still feel uncomfortable, shaped
(modulada); those spaces we
choose to inhabit?   → How do
you fill the gaps between this
(if) missing parts?   ↑ Or how
do you build the continuities?

    ↗ How to we make sense of
what we are when, we – as Alice,
have been form so many different sizes in only one day?

    ↙ Which are the translations,
movements, transits that we
have to make within and between this multiple territories?

    ← What are the tales and sto-
ries that we make in order to
give continuity within this shift-
ing/moving territories?   ↙ How
do we embody this minor becomings within our collectivities?

Memory Is The Virtual Is Duration

by Amit S. Rai

#postcoloniality   #dis/   #place
#neoliberalism   understanding   #positionality
#movement   #translation

My dreams are so exhausting, full of monsters of an indeterminate variety. I can't see what contradictions they are working out. Omnes determinatio est negatio: "Everything depends here on the correct understanding of the status and significance of negativity," says Spinoza.

She lived in the Hackney marshes. By lived, I mean that whenever I would encounter her there it struck me that she was most comfortable in the marshes, she belonged there, thrived there. On a clear day, I would see her and Ginger, her dog, in the distance across the long stretch of football pitches, disappearing into the forest cover, wandering, as I thought then. My mother and I would follow her, slowly re-tracing the career of her play; my mother would be speaking. But I understand now that together we were gathering things, displacing them, re-orienting them and ourselves, intuitively following our actual and potential tendencies and capacities. Her name was Tara Singh, and she was unlike any twelve-year old British Asian girl I had ever met.

But that is just a dream, or a multicultural place branding advert, because this girl doesn't live in Hackney, she lives with her mother in Lahore, Pakistan. And my mother is dead. And so I begin with a confession: this is the outpouring of a failed narrative. I had wanted to write the story of one Tara Singh, resident of Bhopal's old city, whose family had lived there for generations, known mostly for the mathematicians and accountants in various universities and trades through-out Madhya Pradesh state. There was a famous relative from Sehore, who had mastered both chess and kabadi and was a university lecturer in knots. He and Tara, his niece, were very close, they spoke regularly. Tara Singh is also the great grand daughter of the last begum of Bhopal (abdicated circa 1951 – check date). The last female in her family.

But… wait for it… she doesn't know who her family is. That's it! It's exactly where the intermission would be in a Hindi masala film from the 70s.

Anyway, back to failed narratives. I have never been to Pakistan, although friends were helping me to get a visa. But who can disentangle the contemporary anxiety of children going to school in Pakistan today? Lahore is not...I know, I know, and just last week in Lahore Cantt area a primary school was threatened with violence. In dreams that wake me I think I see drones cover the sky over Lahore. "They track our route to work, to school, to the market. We don't know what they are looking for, but there are so many of them over the past few weeks..." she tells me.

Tara Singh likes   Ice cream
                 the marshes   being alone
     drawing   dancing   singing   tinkering
                      dogs

Ginger, her dog, likes   fish curry
frozen yogurt
                      well, any food, really
     running fast   sleeping

To continue my confession: I aimed to write this dream as an unintended dance with indeterminate monsters, ab-sent-presences that exert a virtual force on tendencies and capacities. I imagined something along the lines of a lost proleptic chapter in a planned but apocryphally printed volume on the ethology of Tlön. Was the ethology of Tlön a prob-lem that could be solved by Borges's fictive humanity? In A Contribution to the Critique of Political Economy, Marx wrote: "A formation of society will not disappear until all pro-ductive forces are evolved for which it is wide enough, and new and higher systems of production will never be in-stalled until the material conditions of their existence are hatched out in the very bosom of the old society. Hence hu-manity always sets itself only such problems it is capable of solving; since if you examine things closer you will always find that the problem arises only when the material condi-tions necessary for its solution exist already, or are at least in the process of formation." Is the problem of a liberatory ecology of virtual-actual tendencies and capacities one that can in fact be solved by humanity today?

But then what happens when our problems start assuming the aspect of something more like the plotline of a dsytopic science fiction novel? Every ten minutes Google made £150,000. That was about to change as well. Meanwhile, all Hollywood seemed to churn out week after week were variations on the zombie film. We were living in a time of an imperceptible control, our autonomous data unions used in massive marketing / spying/ speculation schemes, experiments in commoning the value of data repeating endlessly: extraction, value, measure, accumulation, logistics, exploitation.

Fifty years ago in the UK in January there would be 20 species of flower in bloom; today the number is closer to 300. Kobane, Syriza, Moditva, Islamophobia, Islamic state, "je suis…? Je ne suis pa…?" What is a political ecology of identity? There are cold winds blowing in Scotland right now but it's the warmest winter on record. The oceans and their inhabitants are dying and super-exploited. And every ten minutes…

My dreams cut in and out of Hindi (and I wonder how Tara Singh writes Urdu, and which one). I hear Hindi-Urdu film songs in my dreams, dialogues, news reports, short story passages. The language is once again alive in me, it offers me another becoming. To write in Hindi, speak in Urdu: isn't that the dream?

But filmi clichés are all I can muster in the language at the moment. To think, to experiment, to dance in a language is to follow through its multiplicities: the plane of expression.

अतुल जी एक और बात बताने लगे कि अखिलिश ने जो लैंप टाप बाँटे हैं उससे कोई इंटरनेट नहीं चला रहा । सब फिल्म और पोर्न देख रहे हैं । इंटरनेट तो फ़ोन में है । लैपटॉप बिक तो रहा ही है लेकिन एक और धंधा चल पड़ा है । उनसे विडी करप्ट हो जाता है । विडो को ठीक करने के लिए दुकानदार तीन तीन सौ कमा रहे हैं । मामूली प्राब्लम भी आती है तो दुकानदार कह देता है कि विडो करप्ट हो गया है ।

Ravi Kumar, बिजली नहीं ये बैटरी क्रांति है
[Not electricity, this is a battery revolution], Qasba,
http://naisadak.blogspot.in/2013/12/blog-post.html?m=1

[Atulji started telling me about one more thing; the laptop that Akhilesh shares is not used for surfing the web. Everyone is watching films and porn. The Internet is on the phone. The laptops are still selling, but another trade has started: They "window corrupt" phones. To fix the window corruption a shopkeeper will charge 300 rupees. The shopkeepers turn even small phone problems into a case of windows corrupt. (My translation)]

In this scenario of jugaad (workaround in Hindi), the shopkeeper is a sinister kind of tinkerer. I dreamt Tara Singh as a tinkerer, but more like Adam Swartz. That she would develop a tinkerer's knowledge of the world and its processes, an ethical know-how – but then am I able to disentangle a desire of and for myself from the dreams of this character? Is the essence of a character the capacities and interactions of definite tendencies? Which method brings forth the ontological limit of character in art – for instance, figuration in painting, architecture, photography, pop song, literature, film? Does the definition of the tendency require a kind of negation, a clear separation or distinction from other tendencies that remain relatively unimportant? What was the last novel you read in which the protagonist was a collective? Dostoevsky engages in this in The Brothers Karamazov in so far as each voice is always already multiple; Bruce Sterling does this on a less epic scale in a story of co-evolution, "Spider Rose" from Schismatrix Plus.

My sense is that Tara and Ginger are bound up in a collective narrative with the marshes. Except they are not living it as narrative, they are living it through composing together the capacities needed to experiment toward the creative life, that is the tinkerer's life. Let's imagine another world/narrative then, not utopic, but hetero-logic. Like Tlön: a world in which extension is only a momentary limit of flux, and that space in itself has no reality, because it has no real duration. Everything is a verb: sunning, tinkering, negating …negating?

"Spinoza ascribes to his inexhaustible divinity the attributes of extension and thought; no one in Tlön would understand the juxtaposition of the first (which is typical only of certain states) and the second – which is a perfect synonym of the cosmos. In other words, they do not conceive that the spatial persists in time. The perception of a cloud of smoke on the horizon and then of the burning field and then of the half-extinguished cigarette that produced the blaze is considered an example of association of ideas (Borges, Tlön 22 – 23).

The evolution of the ethology of Tlön traversed innumerable enunciations, in which poets and physicists collaborated at a distance, tinkering in their distinct but connected media on the ethology of a possible world. Even as Borges' writings are haunted by negation-as-death, a wild inventionism celebrates another method of writing, of speculating an untimely becoming.

But there is no escaping it: vitalism as the discourse of an experiment in capacities seems to present ready made formulas (untimely becoming, intuition, affect, etc) for an ontological practice of affective compositions. Such an ontology would follow through on the fractal method elaborated by Deleuze and Guattari in A Thousand Plateaus, an n-1 method of exit toward the indiscernible. But one cannot escape the truth that to say goodbye to language, repeatedly, and that too within and against language, is always to understand the power specific to a cliché.

Perhaps they indicate another truth as well, which is that the indiscernible is not a state of being but a movement of becoming. This is not an extinguishing of racial, class, gender, sexual, ability-based forms of identity, becoming is not a sublation of difference, because becomings are formed from the molecular intensities of nonlinear ecologies. Rather, it is in the elaboration of styles of collective individuation that one affirms the changing capacities of the practice one assembles with. This is a matter of elaborating strategy and resonance together. Bergsonian memory is not the enemy. A politics of ressentiment is.

Does the concept of overdetermination move us beyond a Marxist dialectic, to a non-Hegelian dialectic? Macherey writes,

When Marx wrote the famous sentence, "Humanity only poses for itself problems that it can resolve," he was still completely part of the lineage of Hegelian evolutionism. The subsequent history of Marxism would demonstrate exactly in the course of events that a question is not resolved simply by the fact that it is asked. But it is already something significant to pose a question, even if it can promise nothing as its answer. To read Spinoza following Hegel, but not according to Hegel, allows us to pose the question of a non-Hegelian dialectic, but we must also admit, and this is also a way of being Spinozist, that this does not enable us at the same time to answer it. (Macherey, Hegel or Spinoza)

Deleuze also wrote of this declaration by Marx. He took it in a very different direction, away from the lament of the failed answer. As Keith Ansell Pearson notes,

> Deleuze offers a Bergsonian reading of Marx on this point. When Marx says that humanity only sets itself problems it is capable of solving this is not the empiricist, or rather, positivist, trap we might think, since the problems take us beyond what we think we are and are capable of. Marx's thought, therefore, is a vital empiricism. For Deleuze, the history of humanity, considered from both theoretical and practical points of view, is a history of the construction of problems (it is a history of over-humanity, one might say). It is in this excessive sense that we can say humankind makes its own history, and becoming conscious of this praxis amounts to a drama of freedom as the 'meaning' of human life and of its germinal existence (the fact that it lives on and survives only by living beyond itself). In a deeper sense, however, the historical character of human existence is an expression of the elan vital which marks life as creative: 'Life itself is essentially determined in the act of avoiding obstacles, stating and solving a problem. The construction of the organism is both the stating of a problem and a solution' (Deleuze 1966:5; 1988: 16; in Ansell Pearson Germinal Life, 23 – 24).

How then do we determine a well-posed problem? Are well posed questions to be determined, or are they the emergent limits of a practice? A question posed not from the telos of an answer but from the processes it attempts to diagram and experiment with? Is there a diagram in every question? Can methods of questioning follow a diagrammatic practice? Are diagrams of affects even possible? Possible, all too possible.

We can thus dispense with the word diagram, it is too riddled with the history of misogynist points, and mastered topographies. "The geometry of Tlön comprises two somewhat different disciplines: the visual and the tactile. The latter corresponds to our own geometry and is subordinated to the first. The basis of visual geometry is the surface, not the point. This geometry disregards parallel lines and declares that man in his movement modifies the forms which surround him. The basis of its arithmetic is the notion of indefinite numbers."

What compels a return to a political ontology in the time of the new vitalist materialisms of ANT and OOO? Perhaps one way to pose political ontology today is to consider the forms of political practices of such academic formations? The intuition for method draws its differently repeated patterns from the many revolutionary becomings in movements for economic and social justice, free education, and radical democracy. These becomings will have activated the memories and resources of decolonization, queer organising, commoning (long live Bethnal Green's Common House!), anti-globalisation, care, precarity, Anonymous, Guanyem-PAH, Embros to Greenpark in Greece, BlackLivesMatter, Why Loiter, BDS, Kobane? Objects are (de)fetishized of their processes, returning matter to both its morphogenesis and its logistical relations. The processes and dimensions of change of objects and their ecologies are well posed when posed together.

> "Unbelievably, these refutations were not definitive." – Borges, Tlön.

What if Tara Singh's story is not bound up with a "silly"
Hindi filmi reference (it is – the pehlvan [strongman] Dara Singh
is her cinematic uncle, I remember him in Anand [1971], in
a scene never shown, leading his charges in a game of kabadi,
or group wrestling--the failed narrative is Bollywood deriva-
tive without experimentation)? What if her story were found in
fragments in a house in which she eventually became a
hacker ghost, after a life of 500 years, a kind of undead, and
kind of Beatlejuice character. Mad, completely mad.
Bonkers, throwing sporks at people all the time. The spork has
to figure into the story. The invention of the spork.

> "Their books are also different. Works of fiction
> contain a single plot, with all its imaginable
> permutations. Those of a philosophical nature
> invariably include both the thesis and the
> antithesis, the rigorous pro and con of a doc-
> trine. A book which does not contain its
> counterbook is considered incomplete."

In a review (2014, Performance Research, 18: 6, pages
130 – 32) of Jack Halberstam's Queer Art of Failure, J. Paul
Halferty notes that Halberstam's quite optimistic approach to
failure and forgetting is balanced with the understanding
of the negative aspects and affects of failure and loss, such as
unbeing, unbecoming, passivity and masochism. In a
chapter titled 'Shadow Feminisms: Queer Negativity and Radical Passivity', s/he explores (following Bersani) what s/he
calls 'antisocial feminism.' Through analyses of Jamai-
ca Kincaid's Autobiography of My Mother and Elfride Jelinek's
The Piano Teacher, as well as the works of Marina Abramović,
Yoko Ono, J. A. Nicholl and Kara Walker, s/he investigates
feminist strategies that provide potential alternatives to liberal
conceptions of womanhood. Many of these texts emerge
out of queer, postcolonial and black feminisms and offer forms
of feminism that are antisocial, anti-Oedipal and anti-
humanist (Halberstam 2011:125 – 6). The forms of feminism
Halberstam sees in these texts are those that think 'in
terms of the negation of the subject rather than her formation,
the disruption of lineage, rather than its continuation, the
undoing of self rather than its activation' (2011:126). Citing

these works, as well as others, "Halberstam argues that memory and memorialization can provide uninterrupted and cohesive narratives that obscure the many breaks and contradictions of history and the many forms of passivity and unbeing that have formed difficult and uncomfortable modes of resistance" (131).

We are the gatherers of resistances, we will gather them together for all the Tara Singhs, all their extra-human permutations and all their actions' permutations, to come. There is no resistance that can resist the universal appropriation of resistance by critical theory today. But what is the affirmation in this or that practice of resistance? What is resistant that is autonomously affirmative in Tara, Ginger, the ecology of the marshes – marshes we should keep in mind that were completely re-engineered during the "rehabilitation" (or the privatization of the multitudes' commons) of Stratford for the 2012 Olympics? This question would limn the inhuman forces in her collective assemblage, where resistance is not anthropocentric but a strategy of experimenting with overdetermined, extra- and infrahuman forces. We must compose assemblages of solidarity, as Franco Berardi reminds us about the current "crisis" of Greece and its seemingly ephemeral euphoria (crisis for whom – the bankers and the oligopolists?). If Ginger and Tara co-evolve in the marshes, what solidarities form, are made possible, or remain virtual through the explication of their mutual implication?

For Deleuze, Nietzsche "made an affirmation of becoming. We have to reflect for a long time to understand what it means to make an affirmation of becoming. In the first place it is doubtless to say that there is only becoming. No doubt it is also to affirm becoming. But we also affirm the being of becoming, we say that becoming affirms being or that being is affirmed in becoming. Heraclitus has two thoughts which are like ciphers: according to one there is no being, everything is becoming; according to the other, being is the being of becoming as such. A working thought which affirms becoming and a contemplative thought which affirms the being of becoming. These two ways of thinking are inseparable, they are the thought of a single element…For

there is no being beyond becoming, nothing beyond multiplicity; neither multiplicity nor becoming are appearances
or illusions. But neither are there multiple or eternal realities
which would be in turn, like essences beyond appearance.
Multiplicity is the inseparable manifestation, essential transformation and constant symptom of unity. Multiplicity is
the affirmation of unity; becoming is the affirmation of being.
The affirmation of becoming is itself being, the affirmation
of multiplicity is itself one. Multiple affirmation is the way in
which the one affirms itself."

     To affirm becoming is first of all to practice philosophy as a
practice of joyous life, a dance of chance. This affirmation
is also an excellent occasion to bring forth a non-dialectical
difference. Difference as we see in the passages from
Halberstam has largely been subsumed under negativity,
negation, opposition, contradiction, and generally a bad
conscience (slave mentality or representation, same dynamic). Affirmative difference suggests a continuous different-
iation of intensive processes, gradients of functionality, rates
of connectivity, and a multiplicious mutation. This is difference as self-differentiation, given an ecology of far-from-equi-
librium states and processes. This is the truth of being:
becoming different. There is nothing but that, a constant becoming (even when rooted in habit, that "bad" repetition),
that is what being is; a working and contemplative thought,
the world is a unity of multiplicious processes.

> [Heraclitus] saw no negativity in becoming,
> he saw precisely the opposite: the double affir-
> mation of becoming and of the being of
> becoming--in short the justification of being.
> Heraclitus is obscure because he leads us
> to the threshold of the obscure: what is the be-
> ing of becoming? What is the being insepa-
> rable from that which is becoming? Return is
> the being of that which becomes. Return is
> the being of becoming itself, the being which is
> affirmed in becoming. The eternal return
> as law of becoming, as justice and as being.
> (Deleuze, Nietzsche and Philosophy)

Tara is Orlando. Tara, her grandmother, my daughter, my mother/myself are a character in a failed narrative of care. Wolfe's Orlando is a collective character that is an intuition of the unity-in-multiplicity of durations, a series of vertiginous displacements separated by the long dureé of hundreds of years or waves of nanoseconds.

We assemble with the powers of the false in any failure. It has its own ontological status does failure, and so its negation is only comprehended after the affective fact and material force of its intuition. Like a failed revolution – is there any other kind? Yes: a revolutionary becoming.

I found the intuition of Tara's story in a set of photos, but the more I thought of it the more they seemed to present a contradictory, anomalous figure. As if lost in a series of forking paths ("The house is a long way from here, but you won't get lost if you take this road to the left and at every crossroads turn again to your left." The Garden of Forking Paths), we see her in a fancy dress sari at a ball or formal event, uncertain what event, in an art deco hall of endless portals in Churchgate.

We return as if trapped in the bad repetition of a clichéd refrain. Isn't all marketing haunted by a constitutive exclusion? What event arrives from the outside that changes Tara-Ginger-marsh? Is it the violence of marketing (cf M. Cage, Marketing is Violence)?

What is marketing anyway?

> So far, we have considered how marketing can be characterized as operating in either the consumer, business-to-business, or services domains. What is common to all these marketing contexts is that the marketer works to satisfy the needs of customers. However, more recently... there has been a realization that marketing also impacts positively and negatively on society. Let's consider how much the marketing industry contributes positively to society (we consider the negative impacts in Chapters 18 and 19). For example, Wilkie and

Moore (1999) describe the complexities of what they call the 'aggregate marketing system'. We can use the example of how marketing brings together the ingredients of an average European 'continental' breakfast. Consider the individual ingredients, for example, coffee or tea, together with Danish pastries, cold cuts of meat, salad and cheese, muesli and cereals, various fruits, the cups/plates and glasses, the oven to cook the pastries, etc. The distributive capacity of the aggregate marketing system is amazing, especially when we consider that there were over 504 million people in the EU in 2012, each of whom is brought their own unique mixture of breakfast offerings each morning (see CIA, 2013). Broadly, the aggregate marketing system in most countries works well. We're not all starving and we don't have to ration our food to preserve the amount we eat. Of course, there are certain countries in Africa, North Korea, and parts of China where people are dying of hunger, but these countries often experience imperfections in supply and demand because of political (e.g. war, dictatorship, famine) and environmental circumstances (e.g. drought). Therefore marketing plays an important role in developing and transforming society (see Market Insight 1.4). A firm which recognizes the important link between marketing and society and uses it to its advantage is the Italian firm Carpigiani, which makes gelato ice-cream makers. It set up Gelato University in Anzola Dell'Emilia near Bologna, taking in over 6,700 students from around the world. The course fees are low to cover the university's costs and include a voucher to purchase ice-cream-making equipment. Accordingly, over the last three years, Carpigiani's sales have increased by 23% to € 113m...
(Baines and Fill [2014] Marketing, Chapter One).

Follow the logic of the passage: it considers marketing's context-functions-contributions-effects. It posits both an instrumentality and an intrinsic value added to marketing: therefore, accordingly... What percentage of the British population is starving? There are news sources on Google up until 2014; after austerity many more thousands in the UK suffer through chronic hunger. Following Lazzarato, we see that the marketing system considers circulation a potentially strategic form of capital accumulation; the passage above even manages to make the relative lack of absolute starvation in Western Europe an achievement of marketing, itself figured through a telos of perfection between supply and demand. The very development and transformation of society is at stake. What affective atmospheres potentialise this passage, this translation from a standard Intro to Marketing textbook to a history of marketing practices in the UK? The 'object-Other' of empathy (the starving brown or black body) is invoked without being invoked, but even prior to that the question of whether self-interest and empathy are in fact contradictions. Today, the mirror neuron system suggest no contradiction between self-interest and empathy. The textbook covers over the neocolonial politics of (over)consumption willfully: the ecological and human disasters of capitalism haunt this passage – later in the text they refer explicitly to peoples in Africa as lower down Maslow's hierarchy of needs (i.e. in a state of arrested development struggling for subsistence and security) than more affluent societies of the global North. Today, if marketing can be said to have an ethics, this is the ethics of social control, human capital, and relationship management. Radical transnational solidarity translates market segmentation Into the monstrous affects of feminist social reproduction.

Negation is necessary for orientation, is displacement necessary for politics? The question supposes we agree on this last term, but there is a paradox here: for there to be politics there has to be difference, sometimes of opinion, sometimes in representation, or in intensity. Marketing is always an event from the outside; when it captures or modulates, when it measures and typologizes, it is very much in the genealogy of Victorian anthropology. This is the event

127

that would potentialise the narrative forming in between Tara and Ginger, my mother and myself, and our bodies, this text, and the marshes; a negation of the resonances, or perhaps better a corporate affirmation of them in lifestyle categories. To each lifestyle, its own ecology of sensation: the contemporary craze for sensory branding is also an experimentation on the mirror neuron system, opening value channels of accumulation in the realm of affect, as Patricia Clough once said.

And the radical politics of emancipation is also an experimentation in different practices – practices of autonomous value, sense, joy, and radical infrastructures of care and resources. Too often, the pirate kingdom of bad repetitions, and rarely a sabotage of clichés, instead, Microsofts and Burrberrys everywhere. Radical political practices may very well be experiments in sabotage; there is often an assumption of class privilege in the discourse of experimentation, yet developing the bottlenecks in value as non-normative organisational behavior can also be captured as disruptive, intuitive innovation. Or poison the data streams: "like" everything on Facebook, immediately click through every advert, create hacking algorithms of autonomatic noise, exit through the noise.[1]

1   The intuition for this affect-image came out of a conversation with Alexandra Joensson and Cliff Hammett, of the hacker collective Autonomous Tech Fetish based out of Bethnal Green's Common House (http://www.commonhouse.org.uk/).

Where is Home

by Julius

working with women

point of rest

univesit adventure

RESEARCH

MUCH POWER

DIDAO TENDE

study
more

DARK
STREET

LOVE

3 Dis

placement

Displacement: A Molecular Map of Discomforts

by Paula Cobo-Guevara

These modest notes are the result of a molecular mapping working across the microcosms and effects linked to displacement – in relationship to the experience of composing politically and affectively within a new city. The context of this 'arrival' into this new territory is situated from my experience within the construction of a mostly precarious feminist collective. These are preliminary notes resulting from the relationships across a diagram of feelings and affects in the context of experimenting the death of this group.

These lines of text are pretty much situated from a collapsed desire in a body ('my' body), from fatigue and exhaustion. A molecular map – of perhaps – micro symptomatologies. So, in a clumsy way, this is a very modest diagram of mostly draft-like questions and rethorical ramblings around various discomfort(s) within this process; they appear as intuitions, lines of conflict, crystallizations and dynamics of subjectivation on the notions of feeling displaced: collectivelly, individually – but also it's as vectors of possibility and intensity.

Inside (and but also outside the borders of the map): a constellation of different bodies being moved, affected, seduced by a place and by others; their ways/modes of encounters, compositions, decompositions, mutations. The body's capacity to affect and be affected; the ecology of relationships and conversations that made me/us, me/you/we feel moved. The capacity to project a desire – but also the capacity to sustain it, and the capacity to mutate this same image into something else.

One of the molecular elements that I followed within this process was experimenting with high doses of individualism within a collectivity. It's sad passion: the maladie du siècle: anxiety, isolation, enclosure; but also within this same nodes of problematics, the capacity to re-elaborate this negative affect and mutate this collapsed desire into other machine. Hopefuly this map serves as a visualizing tool to further unfold and spur into intervention strategies to deal both individually and collectively with these questions that transverse us in many different ways.

137

A LINE.

Moving and translating from different locations and sub-jective territories, in some cases mobilized by the force of affections, crystallizations, love, networks. Escaping those apparatuses of capture such as the nuclear family, class condition, gender, identity, etc. A flee from those dominant forms of subjetification; perhaps seduced by intense polit-ical moments, colletive endouvers. The potency of experiment-ing 'escape' as a liberating practice – in straight relation to an exit of a deeply inscribed neoliberal subjectivity. In short, actively (and reactively) moving from different milieus of geography, territory, stories; institutional settings, life exper-iences and vital experimentations. Certainly, the most immanent to these common stories is the desire to disarticu-late and re-articulate the forms that configure us creatively, emotionally, socially, politicaly. Experiment the ways in which you relate and navigate life, affects, relationships, networks, friendships, and a myriad of formal and informal vihinculations. We all carry these stories, trajectories, and knowledges – these, deeply shaped by specific forms of subjectivities and identities formed at the core of that what you escaped or fled from, and that under specific lines of conflict appear, out of dust, and activate specific ghosts and fears.

MOLECULAR
EXODUS.

Construct and see which are our territories, which are our worlds, our chaos; the alterities in which we move in; where my body starts, where the other body starts, the forms of contact, of composition. Which one is my terriory? Which one is my clan? My tribe?

POWER.

We can think of displacement itself as a biopolitical diagram, in which all the spectrums of our lives are subject to specific forms of subjectifications and power relationships; from forms of citizenship/non-citizenship, to multiple forms of exclusion and discrimination; to forms of labour and precarity, mistranslations and an infinity of power relationships. We could think of inhabiting as a very concrete strategy of orientation, a technology of situatedness within this process; we could also visualize it as an affirmative pink line, hacking along this biopolitical diagram of power. From a micropolitical perspective, the forms of being affected, bonded, articulated, our capacity of composition, of being moved – with and by other individual and collective bodies, stories, and life experiences.

WALK, FALL,
MOVE.

   Walk, fall, compose: reorient and find forms of (well) being between this shifting relationships, vectors and lines along this biopolitical diagram of relations. Everything feels and looks as movement, as velocity: flows of images, bodies, encounters, shallow information, tweets, likes, networks, cities, continents. Inhabiting fluid lives, fluid cities, liquid societies. Gas runs through our bodies, and the shadows of our individualized lives, and neoliberal habits – these are deeply embodied in the way we act, feel, sense, percive and react. I usually feel disoriented, disturbed or overexcited by (personal) feelings and (collective) affects. How to find sences of orientation? To cross through, and experiment in embodied terms an active practice of situating oneself within a new territory – a new city? We actively encounter with new bodies, friends, loves, political processes, networks and forms of organization. Positioning and movement in this case might relate to articulating, assemblying and weaving old stories with those things and people who are new to come. Walk, fall, move through the city and make everyday efforts to build and develop habits around a series of forms of maintaining and sustaining constituent vinculations and relationships, enabling a series of forms of well-beings.

ENCOUNTER.

How to collectively construct a network that is not only consti-
tuted by affect or pure affinity, nor a space of pure resonance;
but as a dispotif – an institution that allows this same network of
affinity, of friendship, of love, of care to formalize? The lack of
these dispotifs, of this form of institutions leads to states of lethar-
gy; the sad passions. The lack of a solid time-based networks
of care – from families to friends to work – often produces a disruptive state of sensing a continuous form of vulnerability and
fragility, like drifting upon a slippery slope. Yes, this is an active
line of tension – there is also a potency immanent to this moment.
How to follow the molecular path of these affects, and create
something out of that? Enjoying the pleasure of proximity and
experimentation, encounters that are happy and joyful, desireful,
sensible, disinterested. However there's also a constant sense
of tension and ambivalence within the articulation of these new
relational encounters and relationships – sometimes we long
for a sence of belonging, sometimes a more detached forms of
vinculation. There's a phrase that has became heavily reso-
nant for some time and it illustrates in a beautiful way this condition (and contradiction): A subjectivity that is more schizo,
flowing, rhizomatic, having more to do with surroundings and
resonances, or distances and encounters, than ties? Would
it be possible to read from this perspective contemporary attitudes, no longer dissenting againt a disciplinary society and
its rigid logic of belonging and affiliation, but rather against a
surveilance society, with its flexible mechanisms for monitor-
ing and conjugating flows?[1]

FEAR.

A question and concern that constantly appears – almost as a
collective symptom – is, that we constantly feel vulnerable and
fragile within these practices, experimentations and laboratories
of everyday life. This new becoming's habits are produced from
either individual or collective bodies operated as counter – effects

1   Peter Pál Pelbart, Cartography of Exhaustion, Nihilism Inside Out,
Univocal/n-1 publications, 2013.

to the norm and/or forms of normalization, generating mirror effects in some cases. We operate and react with those sketched habits in our bodies, those normalized forms we bring out when there's conflict or when we have to manage interpersonal, collective and/or individual problems. We specially react in a myriad of selfish, individualized ways, when exposed to different forms of power dynamics and relationships. Sometimes we react, tending to flee to the normative, to the institutional, to those places the family has taught you as safe, carrying a certain production of knowings, certain affects. Sad passions. Sad passions, those affects lead us toward disempowering routes, evasiveness, and synical mechanisms of being and relating to our families, our networks, our work… our vital projects. How to unblock these affects? Exit, move, contaminate, create, and compose a way out of the impasse of these specific forms of control over our bodies, our individual and collective capacities of taking back our lives, our worlds – without reproducing an evasive line of flight?

displacing the self — collapse

CRISIS

CHAOS

individualization

incapacity of flow
sensibility

fear
narcissism

Return of the self
envy

BLOCKS

incapacity of
imagination anxiety
apathy

fatigue of
being oneself
guilt

distance

PARANOIA

displacement
desire (?) — necessity

vulnerability

continuos feeling
of vulnerability

Rotaguard

slow speed
semi-porosity
care

collective
giving attention
Listening

Composing
sensibilities, body
changing perceptions

common
narratives

Recomposition
following
loss

semi-porosity

creativity

making new connections

Fragments from Conversations on Leaving, Staying and Claiming Space

by Ninaha

Over the span of a couple months, these conversations
between some of the members of Egzilis Collective took place
over the internet while physically being in Kaunas and Vilnius
(Lithuania), Ljubljana (Slovenia), Murcia and Barcelona (Spain),
Zadar (Croatia), and Philadelphia (USA). Although the core
group and activities take place in Kaunas, the geography of
the people involved changes.
These conversations below are meant to address some
of the issues of being grounded in a place, keeping ties and
trying to organize in uncertain economic, political, as well
as social and mental conditions.

145

3/23/2015
8:50:48 P.M.

DP — DŽEMPERIO POZA

DP   First of all, from what L sent, you get a feeling that lots
of people from Lithuania and Eastern Europe in general
over-individualize displacement and permanent movement.
When in reality, after thinking for some time that I do it myself as well because "I am such way" or "I don't wanna live like
my parents", you come to conclusion that we are not moving for ourselves. Otherwise it would not be so massive, would
not include hundreds of thousands of people moving out of
Lithuania and Eastern Europe in general at the same historical
moment, as if the floodgates had broken. There is no reason
to de-radicalize the problem: what we might think of as a free
choice could actually be a dictatorship of that choice, collectively supported by ourselves.
The refusal to "delocalize" would not necessarily be a return
to conservative thinking where you live at your homestead on
the countryside, little dog by the barn, tens of children and
traditional Oedipal community. Rather, staying might be a radical action – of course, not compulsory for everyone – similar
to a refusal "to want" or "to choose". In other words, to want
and to choose against the currents: there is nothing the status
quo is more afraid of than desires gone astray. After all, it
is also a matter of understanding one's position as an Eastern

European: you're a loser if you stay and you're a loser if you move, so what do we have to lose? Achievers are sleeping with the enemy :))

Agamben, who is somewhat silly, gives us not such a bad tool – the four categories of: possibility, impossibility, contingency, necessity. All the time we are whining about impossibility and necessity ("no reason to stay here, we need to leave"), whereas the goal should be the opposite, possibility and contingency ("it is also possible to live in Kaunas, there is no need to leave it" – there is no need to stay or leave, both are possible). This, I think, is our goal :)

By creating kinds of stability this could happen. Not necessarily through radical space, although establishing a network of squats, social centres and what not would be amazing, but also by establishing and sustaining legal structures, such as legalized squatting or free education in a manner that they don't become a trap for us.

The program I suggest consists of one sentence, "So maybe for once let's do it this way, so we don't need to start all over again? Because otherwise it is basics upon basics".

Two sentences.

> **ME** For me it was interesting to go over some Lithuanian [activist] realities by mapping out what, when, and how happened/happening in terms of organizing, starting the openings. It seems that displacement works in interesting ways. Migration of people also has triggered new innitiatives locally. But maybe it is also necessary to think about this desire and options for 'returning home'.

DP Well, there neither is nor should be any necessity to 'return'.

> **ME** Well, yes, but sometimes there is a desire. For me, quite frequently, whatever the reasons. But, so you're saying that if we make permanent places or free education, it is possible to stay. By starting from more tangible things, what are tools or things do you see?

DP I didn't say this so concretely. I see more tools. One of them would be horizontalization of skills and powers, so that there

would be, paradoxically, less of the 'activist' mentality in activism and life in general: no 'pushers' and no 'passives'. But
this at the moment seems to be the most difficult task for us,
for it requires stepping over so many internalised boundaries.

ME   But staying and inventing these forms
of horizontalization is a 'creative' thing, no? And
always worth of attention. Otherwise, it is
merely a question about the relation of manag-
ers and workers/consumers.

DP Very well worth the effort. Here I also wanted to talk about
irony. I was reading Hocquenghem, he writes "always to be
conscious of power relations and always being aware of them
is in itself another oppressive power relation." :) So this irony,
on which we sometimes operate is often an obstacle. You
have a feeling that any new idea won't work, that bullshit is
being spoken and you obstruct the path towards any change.
For example, in terms of workshops, seeking horizontality,
attracting new people. And this is especially seen in the older
generation. They know everything, they've participated
everywhere and always know that nothing will succeed. :)
Balsas & Liepa's [see below] attitude is pretty good here –
trying out radically new things and ways of acting. But maybe
we're getting off topic too much?

ME   Why? It's all related.

DP Cause we are talking about situatedness
and displacement.

ME   I think we need somehow to displace our
thinking models, and run from activism,
and throw out phobias that beyond the milieu
of your few friends, the whole world is
fucked and so on.

DP Yes. The last segment of this sentiment is especially annoying.

ME   Wanna share something about your experiences in London and expectations and
experiences after coming back to Kaunas?

DP Yes, I can. I don't know how it is in Barcelona, but in
London not all is well; although I were there only for a few
months, a bit more than half a year to put my two stays
together. Basically, I wanted to come back, not only because

there was carefully calculated propaganda coming from Kaunas, but also because I felt completely displaced there. Maybe I didn't happen to be in right places, where things are not built on hot air, as it is in many places in the metropolis. I wanted to be back where the "real struggle" is :) After coming back, a couple months of energy and enthusiasm, and then you need some supplements.

ME I was asking Be Statuso a lot about this mythology or 'carefully calculated propaganda'. What do you think it does in terms of collectivity, situatedness, moving forward? Is it some kind of self-deception or an important 'psychosocial function'?

DP I think there could be even more of that 'self-deception', it does have an important psychosocial function. But it should go parallel with courage and publicness. With what provided us with most joy. And most of these illusions/myths/whatever? Food Not Bombs, September 1st[1], all the public things. Also Sp(i)auda[2], when it is published, when people come to a squat or you go meet the neighbors and you find out that people are already organizing against Šapnagis[3]. So all these processes are going parallel – the more you leave your kitchen, the more myth and more energy is created. Some good thought came, but I will lose it soon.

ME You've lost it?

DP A little bit. About the real action as a source of energy. Something that you can touch when you do something physically, something you're concerned about.

1   September 1st is a big celebration for opening of the new school year for all educational levels. Our collective organized a theatrical intervention on the main street of Kaunas, where Vytautas Magnus University was celebrating the beginning of semester, with a massive imitation concrete block – symbolizing the burden of student debt, and was handing out fliers in the form of Ryanair tickets, suggesting that after the completion of their degrees people will most likely become labor migrants somewhere in the Western Europe.
2   Kauno Sp(i)auda is a regular publication intended for mass distribution that gives expression to activities happening in Kaunas and more broadly, meant to provoke and create dialogue over topics such education, work, and the city. It is distributed freely in a printed and online formats.
3   Šapnagis is the owner of the Žalias Namas (Green House), which is squatted now, but is doomed to be torn down to erect high-rise apartment building. Neighbors started to organize against the plan and small scale cooperation is starting up between squatters and neighbors.

ME Yes, but in regards to publicity, certain caution might be needed. Maybe it is my paranoid machine, but looking at the dozens of public performances and protests in Vilnius over the years, the picture is quite sad if what it all comes down is masturbation in front of the computer screen looking at your own images on popular internet news site. I'm not saying that the situation is the same in Kaunas now, though.

DP Novelty is an important factor, but I'm not sure if it's not given more importance than necessary... Because now, internally and externally we might start feeling pressure "to always come up with some different". It doesn't seem to matter any more that there is a squat, that there is Sp(i)auda. Everything's there. In order. Sometimes, all these talks on transversality and machines and how contemporary political subjects are always 'on the run' overshadow what is, generally, labour of sustaining and entrenching that which works, that which brings joy.

ME And constantly thoughts are circling about what actions could be taken. It seems meaningful now to do it with the house, to deal with the neighbors, if there is something to deal with. It appears that it would be a step not only towards acceptance but perhaps towards some kind of new collective perception that more is possible.

DP It needs to be thought through and acted upon, since the struggle is the knocking on the door itself.
Constantly the same question and the same critique comes up. From different people from our environment, such as: "What is the real struggle, how to know, when you really do it, and when you do it for yourself?", "If we were not here, would anything be happening here at all?", "Without a material basis only nonsense comes out." It seems that most important is to feel "meaning":) And not to feel lonely. Because just when we start feeling that way, we fall back on individual activities and 'I don't give a fuck' attitude.

3/14/2015
3:21:00 P.M.

150

BS — BE STATUSO

ME   In some sense it's interesting, how are we looking at Kaunas, because it seems that there is a lot of little brother syndrome (in relation to Vilnius), which is changing now. What do you think Kaunas' problem is and why does it have such a reputation?

BS   Now I'm trying to think how much this imagination that "things are happening in Kaunas" and repeating it to others, to people in Vilnius in particular, contributed to real doing and acting.

ME   I think contributed significantly, no?

BS   Yes, most likely. But also it is related to this sense of irony, which helps you to survive. In terms of the little brother syndrome, I don't really feel it in Kaunas. The only lack might be perceived is from the cultural consumption perspective. Meaning that in Vilnius it is easier to consume everything: art galleries, many cultural events but sometimes it seems that Kaunas, because of its size and because there is less to consume, has lack of spaces where you would like to go and to be. And it creates groups of people, which start creating their own spaces. I'm thinking here about raves and other such things.

ME   Yes, yes. But this impression that there is some kind of upswing – you think it's 'objective' or 'subjective' (putting aside this shallow categorization)?

BS   Now I'm thinking that maybe this imagination about Kaunas potential is part of our myth creation. This myth allows us to be here and belief in this potential. There are also some objective things (first of all the squat, but also the expansion of the collective, sluggish but existing process of the KSP union[4])

Subjective comes more from the relations with outside, when you reflect those relations. It happens when you talk with

4   KSP is an informal Kaunas Street Performers Union.

displacement

people directly, with people who are part of our collective but live in Vilnius, for example. But it also happens via mailing list, in relation to those who are abroad. What do you think about this subjective dimension? How to define it?

ME   I'm not sure. I'm thinking about this sense of potential, myth, daily practices, interactions, 'community'. I think there is something quite drastically different from usual facebook conversations and debates, when people don't see each other and argue endlessly with one another or create small groups of position. But maybe to come back to this mailing list and people being away. I think there are some interesting examples from the collective when it motivates somebody to come back, or keep in touch, and have this mutually beneficial function without being fully present at any given time in one place. And even if this relationship is fragile it still creates links of engagement, meaning, potential. No?

BS   Yes, partially it localizes you. I think everyone who gets involved, does it because they have some hope for Kaunas. Or, to put it differently, believe in that myth. And then this belief creates certain kind of relationship amongst us, which is not based on leftist ideas alone. And I am quite impressed, that people being very far away or not having enough time to fully get engaged in the core group feel certain commitment. You can see it through the mutual fund.

On the other hand, I think those, who give themselves most into all these things, and probably those who are biggest believers in this myth (or maybe not myth), also always feel very insecure and afraid that suddenly everyone will leave and you will be left alone.

The ongoing joke is who will leave first and who will remain to the last. This fear, however, lately started to disappear for an objective reason – hope, that there will be permanent place to do things and to live, having means to survive, a long time to spend together and make stronger commitments to the collective. The myth played its role. It is not as necessary as before.

ME For me it is interesting and important how to arrange that people individually or in small groups can leave, but a certain kind of institution remains to which you can come back. How to create certain commitment that we can individually contribute to that institution, which becomes permanent, without feeling of guilt when we need to leave.

BS Yes, that would be important to me. But out of nothing you cannot create such structure – you need some kind of material base. In this case, the mutual fund is a first step, which contributes to the creation of such institution.

Another thing is with the core group and the feeling that without you nothing will happen, at the same time certain willingness to 'sacrifice' and stay here. And then, that everyone will pity you, how you sacrificed yourself and stayed. Sometimes I feel this sense of leadership.

ME Do you have any ideas how to deal with it? Be Statuso: Most important is to share tasks, information, skills and to look collectively so that this role is not permanently instituted. But it is not so simple, because clearly there are people with more or less time, and maybe more or less desire.

Yes, time is important of course, but there is a need to create schemes, where professionalization of activism is not created, but rather increasing self-organization and self-sustainability (it's that 'give up activism' critique). On the one hand, there are many illusions that dedicated vanguards will take care of us all. On the other hand, if the changes will be real, they will need massive engagement, even if largely differentiated according to various responsibilities of care people have and so on. But the methods of coordination needs to be discovered where more people can do more things together.

BS When I think about this sense of transience, what matters for me is more than the thought that others might be leaving.

It is things like that I'm still living with my mother (which I know I don't want to), economic circumstances, unfavorable conditions for not having to work or to study. Structurally, it would be possible to achieve, but now I'm thinking that this myth, which was part of this whole creation, might also be an obstacle, because it creates perception that everything needs to be here and now and also I have this fear not to miss out on anything important

Whereas structure – and also setting future possibilities and plans more clearly – would allow to reduce individual anxieties and continue things differently.

ME   In my opinion, if you create a certain base, the moment of letting it go might not mean missing out, but rather something complementary, when we get involved in other things in other places, we may be bringing something back, 'grow' and become more complex etc. We need to take these things into account somehow and try to transgress binary the thinking of here OR somewhere there. This is why I think it is useful to think through these terms of displacement and situatedness in terms of Kaunas and our collective, thinking what kind of practices may be developed to address those issues. In some sense, not to get stuck on street interventions or internal methods of collective improvement, but to think about important knowledge productions in a situation which won't change any time soon (migration, mobility, etc) and which could allow to use it as a set of tools wherever you are.

BS   Don't you think that you are moving towards knowledge production leaving outside some important practices?

ME   No, I'm talking about knowledge production as a tool, which is created not by sitting on the sofa, but through practice, encountering problems. In some ways, if it appears that things are highly precarious but it is possible to do long-term things, we should somehow avoid the romantic vision that we find each other and spend the rest of our days together in one place as one family. The knowledge about how to sustain organizational, social, political and emotional balance may be useful wherever we are and in whatever we do. For me it is interesting how through experimentation we create certain kind of basis to deal with reality. Practice and knowledge are not separate things. One more question that I find interesting to explore is about irony and how it is related to cynicism, which is a different thing, but often the boundaries are quite blurry. Cynicism appears to be abundant in 'radical' circles in Lithuania.

BS I think the fact that we are doing something and we are a collective (where you create certain structures and fight for them) is already a step away from cynicism. I think cynicism comes from the sense of powerlessness and attempts to hide this powerlessness. In our collective of course it exists. But I think in those areas where we feel most powerless, its different.

ME You think something like 'healthy' irony, if it may be called that, contributes to 'harmony' in the collective?

BS I don't know if it contributes to 'harmony' and whether it improves everything. But somehow it helps.

4/29/2015
8:14:00 P.M.

RC — RIOTCUP

ME So first of all a little bit about Kaunas. How about answering this question: 'It is also possible to live in Kaunas?[5]. Possible or impossible?"

5   'It is also possible to live in Kaunas' was a social advertisement by Kaunas Municipality, that was received with controversy by the larger public and has ever since remained part of the folklore when referring to Kaunas in ironic ways.

RC Possible. If you know how. From my experience, Kaunas is really not boring when activities – and people who agree with it – appear. Who agree and takes part in it. Otherwise it is a desert.

      ME Do you think these activities can be sustainable? Should it be a goal? Can there be some kind of continuous culture of activity, where people are not necessarily always the same?

RC I think one of the tasks should be making these activities sustainable and this is among the biggest of challenges. If 'culture of activity' appears that probably already means that it has become some kind of social practice and entered autonomous sphere, which signifies that there is no need of those who are pushers, because people know the ideas and they can continue when others retreat. At the moment it is definitely not the case.

      ME Part of the collective anxiety, though maybe not directly articulated is this permanent moment of 'everyone will leave'...
From one side, there is quite a bit of inner collective strengthening (conflict resolution etc), on the side there is a lack of development towards the outside, so much energy is directed to the inside, which is also fragile. Maybe all that is needed is time. About people from our collective leaving – I don't know if we are ahead or behind. Sometimes it seems that it is a new reality that we've got a chance to test out first. "We", meaning those who live in the peripheries nearest the centers. Globally and locally alike. Yes, maybe somebody will leave. But that is why there is a need to create open structures, where new people could easily take part. Which I am not sure is possible in terms of losing content. But I think we need to get used to instable lifestyles and to changing social networks (here I mean people) and to high level of mobility. In terms of a collective's inside/outside, I think

both are needed. Lately I've been thinking a lot
about collectives/movements and how much
they depend on personal relations among their
members. On the one hand, it is important
to always reflect and analyze them collectively.
On the other hand, there is a negative side,
when the inside centers on itself, the stronger
the familiarity with eachother becomes, the
more the circle starts to close and it becomes
harder for new people to join in without
strong personal relations with at least someone
in the collective. I would put these questions
for now into a category of 'existential', because
I don't really know the answer. But this new
reality when there is no stability, are we victims
in it or the agents? Does the Lithuanian
context prove that people here are more willing
to move? If you make here somehow
how you want it then you don't really need to
go anywhere?

RC I don't know, there are always pluses and minuses. We can
be both, I guess. On one hand, the good hand of the state
disappears, dehumanizing paternalism and numbing stability
(25 years in front of assembly line and pension afterwards).
On the other hand, instability may create exactly the same
consequences for other reasons.

ME Kaunas has this reputation that is transient.
People leave. There are large student populations, but after a few years they leave. There
is migration out of country as the whole
and out of the city of Kaunas in particular.

RC Maybe not to the same extent now, lots of people moved
out already. But yes, emigration is one of the crucial aspects, especially since there is no immigration.

ME How to situate yourself and how to do it
in the movement through network and continuity, as in your example now in Ljubljana. This
might be the 'nice' kind of emigration. But
as we all know, most of it is not pretty when you
work in the fish factory in Norway or strawberry

fields in the UK. I think one of the potential practices we can work towards is making 'exchanges' based on our interests, where we go to places and people from those places spend more time here. Some circulation may be healthy and networks of international support. It happens somewhat but could be developed further.

RC   Perhaps, but this need comes up for reasons that are not personal. Rather they are the personally felt consequences of larger process (migration and other politics). It is true that in Lithuania there isn't lack of stagnation and sometimes you simply need to run in order not to be psychologically crushed.

ME   Exactly

On guilt...Very Catholic concept, but while talking to others it appears as a feature about leaving the place, when there is a commitment to be in place and try out continuity.

RC   Yes, unfortunately, there is such a feeling. Very fucked up feeling. It seems that this is one of the aspects we need to be working on and find some kind of synthesis.

ME   Because if your commitment is based on guilt, sooner or later it will end up in resentment. Related moment is the core group within our collective. Inevitably there appears internal habits, conversations, vocabulary, which become difficult to communicate. But commitment can still be done over distance and more experimentation is required to see how it can be done. Because this reality of displacement is not about to end.

RC   Ok, it's not only guilt. For me, there is a certain enthusiasm to show support and try to participate. Guilt would disappear if I knew that there is sustainability, but at the moment everything is still so fragile. So it always seems that even when one person leaves it affects the whole collective and the collective's productivity.

Exactly, this reality won't stop any time soon. And any ways, it seems, that there will be more of this reality.

ME Irony is related to all this somehow, at least in our context. Irony is always close to me. I think good irony has more subversive potential when facts displayed in the cold manner. But yes, there is a thin line between understanding/misunderstanding, irony/cynicism.

5/14/2015
7:42:51 P.M.

L — LIEPA, B — BALSAS

ME What do you think about that phrase 'It is also possible to live in Kaunas.' And a few words about Kaunas stereotypes. Why the image is so unclear? And is it from inside or the outside? Or maybe its all old news? Stereo-types about the 'heart of Lithuania', conserva-tivism, purity, etc...

L And the streets full of potholes.
Why it is like this, so far I cannot answer, but thinking about inside/outside, there is adoption of outside opinion, if not as a 'real' thing, at least the jokes about Kaunas. You hear that Kaunas, and even more so people in Kaunas, are this or that and finally, even if you disagree, it becomes part of the small talk that you take on.
In terms of old news, I would say that now is the new trend to say that things are HAPPENING in Kaunas.
B I don't remember the image from 'inside'. From outside it is dual. On the one hand, when you come back from Vilnius first of all you start to feel that at least in the center there are more tough guys, generally grey (color-wise, not in terms of values), crouching people. On the other hand, Vilnius' colors disguise emptiness. Lithuanian-ness is something that prob-ably comes out more in Kaunas.
L When I was living in Kaunas I didn't feel less in center than in Vilnius. Vilnius never was something special and Kaunas something shitty. And now also I can't say that I feel very strong desire to live somewhere else, abroad, somewhere more global.

displacement

B If I feel some attachment to specific places they definitely cannot be measured by the width of Kaunas, Vilnius, or even more so, Lithuania.

L Here and there it is equally lonely if there are no people around whom you trust and can do something with enthusiasm. During the Karnival[6] we've talked to someone who migrated to London and it didn't sound as if the squatting tradition and current squats, for example, create something more extraordinary than here. And she said that she really wants to start living here again, that she wants to get involved because here is a vibe, so to speak.

B I also, lately, try to live according to this "Where, if not here? Who, if not you?..." discourse. In addition, I'm thinking of transfering my studies to Kaunas in the fall if I don't need to pay anything

ME Let's talk a bit about mythology.

B Is it a Greek mythology, Ricouer's mythology, Egzilis mythology?

ME You choose.

L What is there to talk about. When you don't see things in action only read letters, everything looks very nice and good. The negative side of it is that expectations coming from this imaginary community do not correspond with reality. At least this is what people in Kaunas say. But the image, that things are really happening in Kaunas, certainly exists.

B I happily reproduce that mythology in Vilnius, taking it as an example that it is possible to do things and good things can come out of it. I know that when activities of the collective intensified, more problems appeared. But I can understand someone from the collective who says 'I feel shitty but now I am the happiest in my life'. In Vilnius it is easier to live comfortably. Kaunas, it seems to me, is not that comfortable and maybe it is its advantage. In Kaunas (and maybe it is a blunt statement) if you want to actualize something, you need to do it yourself. And if you not going to do it, you need to look for others who are doing it. I don't see any problem with

6   Kaunas Karnival was a weekend-long event in May 2015 which brought people from the ECE region engaged in squats and social centers for getting to know each other, workshops, discussions and parties.

creating mythology and exaggeration, because searching for people to act together in Vilnius for a year, there was no chance whatsoever to reach similar intensity as with Egzilis in Kaunas.

ME Can you tell a bit about your experiences being between Vilnius and Kaunas and about possibilities of being involved over distance.

L To be involved over distance is possible, but it is much more complicated and requires much effort. It is much harder to support activities in Kaunas as part of your everyday life: because you won't meet these people in the city, not going to go to their home, won't eat lunch together, won't see them at the university. Practically, when you want to feel this relation, you need to make a special effort, which automatically doesn't emerge from your daily life.

ME Can you say a few things about the importance of place?

B Space seems to be essential and struggle through space seems to me most solid one at the moment and then the crucial methodological/practical question for anarchism becomes how to acquire widely recognizable, widely adaptable and relatively dynamic forms of continuity. So space, it seems, materializes ideology and it is an institution in itself thus different space or differently practiced space foresees some kind of continuity and possibilities to produce and reproduce practices which are necessary or compatible with it. I don't know if I'm able to imagine continuity in any other way right now.

3/17/2015
7:39:51 P.M.

N — N

N So where would you like to begin and for what?

ME Well, there are few things for why, but mainly for the reasons of thinking through what does it mean to try this (mainly) locality-based collective when this locality is hard to get oneself attached to, for the most of us.

displacement

N   Well, it's not easy for me to say too much on the state of collective as there's been a lot of developments since I left. Well let me try. For example, I wrote someone an email about the burnout workshop. The idea of having a burnout workshop is not a good omen for me. I think it's probably one of the most convoluted concepts of the activist milieu. It makes me think of organizing as an after school sport, the race you can get tired of and then the whole thing of dealing with personal life and having a meeting once a month to focus on these issues is funny to me. because it seems from my experience that the bread and butter stuff is what keeps real shit together in the first place
I brought it up with some people out here who have never been involved in radicalism and it just sounded really bizarre to them. Like how can you burnout? you have to keep on living I guess I'm just saying the important thing is having people that actually have your back and know how to deal with shit when shit gets very real

> **ME**   But part of this having people who can have your back is about having relationships.

N   YES!

> **ME**   And some of the strength and stress in Kaunas is exactly about that. Feeling that you start having something more solid and that it can go away and decompose at any minute. And how to deal with this.

N   Well it can't. not if its solid. there is certainly no easy resolutions of course but like say with my new comrade Kalid or Charlie who runs a Nigerian grocery next door, it's like they are pissed off and really angry about life here and are amazingly supportive and welcoming. I just met Kalid and he's really concerned about my well being and trying to teach me how to deal with the job. We don't have a method of revolutionary organizing but first of all the relation won't die because it's based on a practical dependency not to say we don't talk lots of shit about American imperialism in North Africa but it's grounded on him actually helping me out. These are the relations I'm interested in. And as I say with the New York radicals who started coming around, they have been in different political groups in NY over many years. These groups often amount to little to nothing, recruiting MA students. They are aware of this and more connected than most with what is and is not going to work but they still have a disconnect in terms of what will motivate us to get organized in more disciplined way. this also takes time. I really don't care to be around self-proclaimed radicals. They get stuck in PC land, are not down and don't know how to deal with money. Absence of intuition. And then they come by, make a mess and I have to do clean up because they don't actually talk with people outside their circles often, e.g, with my comrade Egypt who is an amazingly perceptive Trinidadian Muslim, who does street photography. I introduced him to this New York guy and then New York guy decides that he has to declare his entire political agenda as though it's just a number to recruit for a political project then I had to restart relation with Egypt and it took a while for him to realize I was down. Now we go to park and he raps in Arabic and we talk about how the police and politicians are the crusaders, social autism of intellectuals – it's not their fault.

ME   Ok, I see what you getting at, but you don't tell me much about all this thing in Kaunas.

N   Well I really don't know so much right now.

ME   I mean, on the one hand you value it somehow. This can be seen in your emails etc. But on the other it could be seen also just self-proclaimed radical group. I'm not interested in what's happening right now. I'm interested in your relationship and whether you think there is a way to keep it. Or is geography of where you are here and now is the only way.

N   Well, I think it's a different situation out there a bit, a small bit, but also very similar to here. I very much keep this relationship and do consider Lithuania a home. I learned a lot from over there, it completely changed my relation with America and I probably wouldn't have been hanging out with the people I'm hanging out without having spent time. It's hard to do counter-factual histories though. :)

ME   Ok, but for me some questions would be coming back to your burnout workshop comment, which I feel you have some hostility towards, or at least scepticism. So on one hand, there is a collective attempt at something collective, on the other, there are individual relations that you have or we all have. It is a question of whether it is important to do some collectivity and maintain it. Otherwise, we can reduce to bread and butter and leave it to organic composition or decomposition.

N   I haven't seen effective political organization in my life; or when I have, it disappeared in the duration of moments. I also am discontent with what I have in many ways as life is not easy and there is a lot of pain or let's say pleasure too. I'm discontent with both.

I'm meeting with a black construction workers group in North Philly next week and have a new contact with a Latino militant group who's organizing laundromats in Harlem. Maybe I will see something there. What do I see so far in Kaunas collective? Well I haven't been happy with the mailing list because the only time people talk with me is as political member and it was giving me very much, it seemed very formal and at this point rather have more personal emails with people I miss and see the gritty moments.

I want to come back, why? (I'm the question person now). So it was really cool to hear about how Sp(i)auda was distributed in the schools but these kinda things take quite a lot of dedication. I remember the Greek guy out in Vilnius talking about handing out their magazine and they did that for a long time and kids started to get to know them after a while and they made contacts but this isn't the direction you're looking for on this discussion.

Back to me. for example, I've imported the Taškas[7] style here with the house where people come by all the time and we make food as social space, this is a connection with the group that has impacted me.

ME   For me it seems that you are somewhat avoiding this question whether these not bread and butter directly related collectivities are

7   Taškas was an infoshop/social space in Vilnius in 2013 – 2014.

meaningful or not – and if they are, as in case of Kaunas, these questions of relationships, migration, etc are important. There are bigger political questions, and they are intertwined, but then the scepticism towards maintenance of collectivity for me sounds to lead to another direction.

N Hmmm okay. Well for example to have a house where I can go to there. To have people that can help me out. These are all very important and I don't take them for granted, especially having spent so much of my life in NY where you can really fall into the despair of having no one at times. So when we're talking about fragility of our collective I'm contrasting this with the fragility of collective forms in NY. In contrast Kaunas seems very together. I don't have much worry on that front. Now in terms of things changing or people going and coming these questions, well, I wouldn't say I have any grand ex-pectations for what will happen and it seems more often than not to not to start the parade with banners that were going to six flags of America and getting tired with celebration before we begin journey. There are bread and butter issues that keep people together I'd say, i don't know. As I say, its not so easy to "evaluate" situation over there. Lots of activity and energy, something is turning people on. I can't name vices and virtues. But you say people are really concerned about the group dissolving or something?

ME Yeah. I mean that's why these conver-sations seem to be relevant. Maybe so far they are not very elaborate. But there is this feel-ing in the air that people will go away, some are more active than others, etc. So in the end what it comes down to is whether it is a matter of particular composition of a group or cre-ating certain means of 'institutional reproduc-ibility'. Also the question, when it is geo-graphically dispersed whether it makes sense for people to be maintaining some kind of ties and how it may or may not help the things keep on going.

N Well the group seems to parallel Kaunas well enough in terms of a disturbance of composition.

> **ME** As you know, there isn't much tradition of doing something together in this kind of more 'radical' tradition. So there are quite a few individual voices, but they never move into something that is at least symbolically materially based (like the mutual aid, or collective fund we've started). It starts to make a difference in terms of openings to do things more effectively.

N Ah yes, like the mutual aid collective fund is great idea and it means if someone gets fired or whatever they will have the resources to rely on. Classic union set up of the old days and hence can be more militant so there you go.

> **ME** And for you personally, what role the existence of this collective or its proto-forms, helps you – or not – to feel at home, to develop things, or to have some space to work through things in LT context.

N I mean it's certainly more attractive to come back with a collective there. I can't imagine if I had to go to Vilnius and it was the same scattered shit. I would have certainly had second thoughts on coming back to LT, that is for sure. Between the countryside and Kaunas it's quite good.

I'm Out the Door

by Alan W. Moore

It feels silly to say, but this morning I was driven from our
apartment by Pepita, the aggressive cleaning lady who comes
every Tuesday. She arrived this morning earlier than we
agreed upon – she has been pushing the time earlier for a while
now. And I was more foggy than usual, having lost sleep
from nightmares. These concern my storage, the masses of
stuff I have in New York City and Milwaukee. In the dream
this stuff was for some reason all on display; people were pick-
ing through it, asking if they could buy things. "These are
duplicates," one man said. No they were not; each one was
different, a female performance artist of the early '80s.
Well, why not sell them to me anyway? Meanwhile, his friend is
putting things in his bag and walking out.

167

This was one in a more vivid set of regular nightmares
about my storage of stuff from the old times, about the 2 or
300 boxes left over from times I can barely recall – down-
town NYC in the 1970s and '80s, the world of art and culture
which now has some kind of historical interest, in a growing industry of the imaginary past compounded of collective
institutional guilt and the curiosity of the young in a city
that has systematically destroyed the grounds for creative
production existent during those years. I have a lot of
work to do now on two new books about the resistant world
of European squatting. Now it's the tedious work of editing.
Pepita was so bustling, so complaining, so pushing on me this
morning that I couldn't stand it. I simply couldn't stay in
the place. I had to get out, even without a shower, only a spot
of deodorant, and rush off to anywhere. I always feel weird
in the Spanish public eye, so different from the U.S., especially
in this fiercely bourgeois barrio of Madrid, this rich person's
neighborhood in a foreign country. The well-dressed old ladies
with their 1950s hairstyles in the tea room I landed in, the
gentlemen dressed like showroom dummies. Me dirty, un-
combed, in my Portland grunge shirt which lays to hand,
just to get the hell away from the house. I'd so much rather be
living in Lavapiés, the barrio of the immigrants. All the cool
people I know live there. Which is in itself a problem. But I am
here, in my lover's apartment in Salamanca barrio, among

the rich, an undisguised foreign hippie – or, as they say here, "an alternative type."

I believe in physical causes rather than psychic. Those nightmares were surely due to a late night dinner of duck liver, an angry animal spirit reminding me of karmic burdens. But this morning I was beyond unfocussed – I was trembling with agitation as I sipped the tea. In a half hour I had a physiotherapy appointment for my failing knees...

I know that really, this is nothing. A momentary attack of bourgeois neurosis by a confirmed Luftmensch set back in his study of leftist minutiae. Try penury, joblessness, and eviction for a taste of real dislocation, or a refugee camp with jihadis on your ass. And, finally, I must admit, this dislocation was productive. Marc asked me for a text on dislocation, and here it is. As a real live expatriate, now nearly five years gone from any real U.S. engagements, I work this dislocation all the time. This tension of dissatisfaction, of never being at home, always a little off center, sitting on the edge of the chair or leaning it back, a little disgruntled ("it's good, but I've had better"), is continual. Like the hatred of the quotidian, whatever its form, the craving for novelty, the delight in being startled, and engaging the weird which even as a child drove me into the world of art.

Do I miss North America? Yes. I sure don't miss the dismal rounds of U.S. politics, nor the disinterest in my weird opinions and research no one ever cared about. I am nostalgic for the country, which is beautiful, and the linguasphere, which I enjoy and can move and play in easily. But now I really have nowhere to go back to. Places I have lived and loved in, even for decades, don't need me. They aren't home. I'm gone.

But it's not bad. This dislocation, the work of a lifetime both given and chosen, has been very useful to me. It has become somehow the grounds of my being. With it, through it, I can produce. I can do things that I think matter, that contribute somehow, that can be part of a bigger change, a necessary wave of a different life. I feel located in history – historian is my chosen work, after all – in that my work could mean something in the future when I'm gone. It's already in there, in the record.

I wrote most of this with a pen I bought at a newsstand. I had fled the apartment without one. If I didn't have a pen and paper, I'd really be dislocated.

Syncretic Space and Transversal Parties: Friday night with Calais Migrant Solidarity

by Claire English

Calais Migrant Solidarity[1] is an activist collective established at the end of the Calais No Border protest camp in 2009. Some of the solidarity work it does could be considered charitable, and there are on-going arguments about how to negotiate our activism alongside our critiques of the big society and its model citizens. The list of activities currently being carried out include; free English classes, free basic legal advice (outlining options available for those that wish to make a claim in the UK and those that intend to live clandestinely), workshops running through the questions the UK Border Agency ask during the asylum application process, sleeping in front of the squats and encampments (the press calls these the 'jungles') to prevent immigration raids, the occasional temporary housing of injured people and minors, organising demonstrations against the mayor and other ministers when they meet in Calais, myth-busting leaflets about what the International Organisation of Migration (IOM) actually provides if you agree to return to your country of origin, and twice a year taking over the meal provision usually done by the charities when they have their 6 week break. The group is constantly revising what is 'too charitable' to be considered solidarity work which is a whole paper in itself, but I think that gives you a vague idea of the activities and ethos of the collective. I'm writing as an activist who has spent over a decade organising in campaigns against immigration controls in both Australia and the UK, and as a PhD student writing about the ways that activists negotiate questions of gender and race in migrant solidarity projects.

At one point during my visits to Calais, activists were sleeping and organising in a place called 'the office' which was also used as a place to hang out during the day with groups of migrants that didn't usually interact with each other whilst undertaking the activities listed above. During the day, the

171

1   Calais Migrant Solidarity is without doubt one of the most challenging and rewarding collectives I have ever had the privilege of being involved with. It's an on-going project that is fairly well established in terms of funding and activist footfall, more information can be found here: www.calaismigrantsolidarity.wordpress.com.

office was usually occupied by around 80 per cent migrant men (Afghans, Egyptians, Sudanese and Eritreans, though this varied) and 20 per cent European anarchists/activists, spending hours chatting, drinking sweet black tea and checking emails.

WE ARRIVED IN THE
AFTERNOON…

A friend I'd made through feminist politics was keen to visit Calais with me, she was considering spending an extended amount of time doing solidarity work there and wanted to see what it was like. We arrived in Calais to the freezing blustery wind, I'd forgotten just how bitterly cold Calais is in the middle of winter. The wind lashing off the coast made the small, impoverished border town feel miserable, even more so than usual. With barely enough French to order a taxi (always a source of embarrassment for me, and yet I do not take an evening class… It's hard to take an evening class specifically so that you can better understand the bitter edges of the EU migration regime, my ignorance is a buffer I allow myself) we gave ourselves a slightly bewildered start to our trip at best.

It was going to be my last trip to Calais for probably a good deal of time, I was in the early days of pregnancy and staying in a hotel and was making the trip for specific reasons. I had two things I needed to work out, I wanted to give my friend a sense of project and finish my interview with a charity worker who had volunteered to give some context to my PhD research. The short timing of our trip made it hard to get a feel for some things happening in Calais. Mostly people from CMS were spending their days walking the streets looking for and opening squats, or in the office, which was the last rented space CMS had left that hadn't been closed down due to Health and Safety regulations, holding an 'improper licence' or some other arbitrary loophole.

We went to the food distribution first. The charities provide a free meal in the evenings. The meals contain barely enough calories to sustain a child let alone an adult, but the food is free and it is warm. As two new women sitting with

CMS activists, we got a lot of stares. It is seemingly partly interest and partly curiosity, 'Why do so many activist women come to Calais? To do what? To hang out with us at food distribution? What do they want?' says the look. The look is almost always silent and often unbreaking. It is usually followed by shouts of 'Hey, are you No Border?' (are you an activist?) or if you ignore them 'Hey, are you cop? Are you journalist?' and will keep going until you reply. What has been deemed the 'Calais stare' is something that is usually un-threatening, receiving it feels like being a stranger in someone else's space, and once you are known you don't get it anymore. It could be read as sleazy, and sometimes for some people it is, but usually not actively. If alcohol is involved (many migrants say that they never drank alcohol until they got to Calais, but now it can be a big part of being trapped and unable to cross) then it can be the beginning of someone getting in your space, especially if they don't speak enough English to communicate with you, if you don't look away fast enough then it might be interpreted that you want them to come over – kind of like being picked up in a nightclub. Again, it can be uncomfortable but rarely, if ever, aggressive. It's quite hard to explain. There is a lot about Calais in this stare, our attitudes towards it and what your relationship to in-dividuals and the place itself is like after you have been around long enough that you don't really receive it anymore.

The other thing worth noting was that this trip took place in the aftermath of France legalising same-sex marriage. You could tell this, because all over Calais, but particularly in the area towards the port, near food distribution, there were activist stickers on every pole, in French, calling for Calaisians to stand against the change. There were pictures of stick figures (one man, one woman) and 'Say no to homo marriage' written on them, and another set with a picture of a baby's face that stated 'For me I need one mother and one father. No to gay parenting'. There was not an organisation listed, but they were in a particular style that I imagine is similar to other propaganda put out by the same people- a type of brand-ing. They added to the sense that Calais is a pretty hostile place for Others- even those with a EU passport...

LATER, THERE WAS A PARTY…

On a Friday evening the office is opened to the public for a party. It is like any other party I have been to in that some people who claim they never drink are drinking quite a lot, and some people who always drink a lot are drinking a lot, and even those who do not drink are clutching one in their hand like a weapon drawn- alcohol is a strange symbol of to-getherness. It clumsily announces itself as a solidarity party on a sign on the door, and as I have learned over time soli-darity is uncomfortable, even or especially if it is working.

I am there in my usual discomfort, part activist and part researcher, my nervousness hovers behind my conversations with local families and migrants and the other militants. It is uncomfortable for me, because as a scholar activist each moment of my ethnographic work includes a series of important relations; how we as scholars relate to ourselves as activists, how we see ourselves in relation to other activists and the kinds of relationships we build' (Pulido in Hale, 2008:350). So I feel a pressure to be a good scholar, a good comrade, a good member of a good project. The front room of the office is warm, which is of vital importance, the frosty winter winds screeching across the freezing coast-line has hurried us all inside together. The atmosphere is thick as usual, so much complexity in this space where we attempt to communicate in broken English, or by an appoint-ed translator, making conversations either long and involved or short and of body language alone. The conversations are friendly as people talk about their favourite Egyptian food, why tea should always be served black and with lots of sugar, who wants a haircut, who wants to play football in the park tomorrow.

One of the local French families arrives, their housing estate is only a few minutes walk from the office, and they are here to see Mark. 'Where is Mark?' they want to know. Mark is an activist who is regularly in Calais, he is handsome and kind and committed, in a No Borders meeting last month we joked that he is either perfect or a police infiltrator. He had visited the local family's home to talk about the increased police presence in the area since the No Borders office opened and the family like him. Mark says members of the family have agreed to send a text message to the office phone if they notice the police are sitting in their vehicles around the corner as they occasionally do, taking photos and writing notes about the office attendees. In return we will try to warn them if we see the police first, that way they can avoid police threats against them for street drinking or playing loud music or smoking spliffs outside in the afternoon. Mark emerged from the kitchen (he was attempting to make a meal for everyone out of the expired canned goods in the kitchen, 'most of the cans do not have maggots in them' he reassured us all). He greeted each of the four the family members by name.

A Sudanese man, Samad, who has been in Calais a number of weeks and is well known to the Calais Migrant Solidarity activists (partly because he is sleeping with a French activist and stays in her bunk most nights) poured the family a drink and looked shy but slightly pleased when the father asks in French where his girlfriend is. I am introduced to the family as someone who has been coming to Calais for 'a long time', but we do not know any of the same people as the French people I usually stay with are involved in the New Anticapitalist Party and do not live on housing estates, and they seem to come to the office less these days. The older son gave me one of his beers and I cannot tell if perhaps he is flirting with me, but I do not mind. He is about 15 and looks tough, if I was a teenage girl at a disco I would dance the other way.

In truth, you could not call this a 'safe space', there is too much alcohol flowing and some people are seriously intoxicated, lots of people do not know each other very well, no one has attempted to discuss any 'rules of engagement' for the office but for me, this is a beautiful night. The office is a space that attempts to bring many worlds of Calais in to the same room, even just to talk about how cold it is.

Ruth Wilson Gilmore talks about the prisoner solidarity groups and spaces she organises in as a chance for marginalised people to become effective political actors by bringing together those that have seemingly irreconcilable interests and backgrounds. She uses the term desakota, a Malay word that means 'town-country' and refers to places that are hybrid (or syncretic is her preferred term as hybrid implies originally pure origins) and are neither urban nor rural. Gilmore's suggests the goal of this kind of thinking is to 'compare political, economic, territorial and ideological valences that distinguish, and might unite, disparate places shaped by external control or located outside particular development pathways' (Gilmore, 2008:35). In her work about prisons, these spaces are occupied by prisoners, prison abolitionists, family and friends of those in prison and the poor and racialised communities most affected by the social and environmental degradation associated with the construction of prisons. These diverse communities work together as a mix, 'composed of places linked through co-ordinated as well as apparently uncoordinated forces of habitation and change' (36). Within these desakota organising communities there is a 'respatialization of the social' so that communities previously united around race or ethnic categories form the basis for syncretising previously separate political movements, 'illuminating shared problems without by-passing particularity' (44). The concept was picked up by Robert Alvarez to discuss the political economy of bricks and mangoes across the US-Mexico border as a way to move away from state-centric accounts of the border, emphasizing instead the way that both mangoes and bricks are shaped and reconstituted by processes of movement (Alvarez 2012).

It is processes of movement that have brought these various transborder people together here in the office, but the stark reality of the haves and the have-nots rears its head at the end of the night. The poverty that envelopes so much of Calais, especially the impoverished area where the office is located and the abandoned factories by the port where the migrants sleep, makes the end of the party feel bitterly cold. The Calais Migrant Solidarity activists, and those who share a bed with them, eventually make their way to their bunk beds, and the French families roll back to their flats down the road. I wasn't awake long enough to say goodbye to the migrants, the only ones that had to brave the wind and the cold in order to sleep, separating in to ethnic groups again and returning to their designated jungles. A party is just a party, but making a convivial place to chat, to reproduce ourselves, to think collectively, does more than initially appears – at least we hope.

Alvarez, R. (2012). "Borders and Bridges: Exploring a New Conceptual Architecture for (U.S.-Mexico) Border Studies." Journal of Latin American and Carribean Anthropology 17(1): 24 – 40.

Gilmore, Ruth W (2007) Golden Gulag: Prisons, Surplus, Crisis, and Opposition in Globalizing California. London: University of California Press.

Hale, C., Ed. (2008). Engaging Contradictions: Theory, Politics and Methods of Activist Scholarship. FAQs: Frequently (Un)Asked Questions about Being a Scholar Activist. Berkley, University of California Press.

Making a Parallel Society Visible through Community Theatre

by Sara Larsdotter Hallqvist

OR: CONTEMPORARY
HISTORY WRITING ABOUT
A PARALLEL SOCIETY
AND POSSIBLE WAYS
OF RESISTANCE –
GIVING UNDOCUMENTED
MIGRANTS VOICE AND
VISIBILITY THROUGH
COMMUNITY THEATRE

I applied for asylum when I came here, and my demand
was rejected. "Ok", they said, "now you have to go back
to your country." And they told me to come in and sign some
documents. But I said no. I am not going back to Africa,
unless you have listened to my problems. If you don't listen to
me, I am not going. "Ok", they said, then we give your name

to the police". And they did. The police arrested me, and sent me to the detention center in Åstorp. Åstorp detention center. That is where I spent 10 months. And then they deported me to Africa. They didn't say anything, they just came. "Today, we will make you leave Sweden." I said ok, but I want to see the documents first. They said "no". They put handcuffs on my hands, on my legs, on my stomach. Yeah, they have something like this, they put it on the stomach. But they didn't show me the documents. We took a private jet, in Malmö airport, me and six police officers. Just me and six polices to Africa, in a jet. And we went to Africa, and we came back to Malmö again. Yeah. Because the country they sent me to, it's not my country. I'm not from that country. So when we arrived there, the country didn't accept me. And the police officers took me back to Malmö again.

You have to always make it clear in your mind – this is not your country. Like me – this is not my country. This is their Sweden, their country. This is their Sweden, their country, and the country is ruled by the police. The police have the rights to do anything. They are always right. So if you want to live here, just go by their rules. Do what they want, just follow them. Don't talk to them, they are not going to listen to you. This is their system. This is their country. This is their law. And their law says they have to kick you out.

You get on the bus and you sit down. People see you are black. They see the seat is free, but no one will come and sit beside you. The seat is there. There are lots of people on the bus. The seat is there, free, they can see it. But no-body... they prefer to stand. And me... I don't care. If you like to sit, you sit, if you don't like to sit because I'm black... then stand! It is your own problem. If you sit down, do you think I will do something to you? Do you think I want to talk to you? If you prefer to stand, rather than sit beside me, it's your own problem. That's the way I see it.

I changed my address like twelve times during the year I was here. Because when you live in an apartment or a flat, and you live without papers, they can ask you to leave any time they want. This is really bad. I was living with people that didn't know that I was living without papers; I didn't tell them. Mostly I don't tell people, because you cannot trust them. And when they realized I lived without papers, they asked me to leave, because they were afraid... they thought I would put them in danger. For some time, I was without a house. I was really heartbroken. Then I found a new place to live, a room in an apartment. With some really nice people. They made me feel good, and welcome. I was so surprised that they let me live with them, without knowing me. And they gave me the keys to their house! I didn't feel I was welcome to Sweden before, but after that I was really much more... like... I mean I feel better to be here, in Sweden. Before I couldn't trust anyone. But the love I got from them... I just try to trust people again. And that was a really positive thing that happened to me, and that changed me. That key they gave to me, maybe they have forgotten, maybe it was something very small to them. But to me, it was like they gave me the keys of heaven.

I think there are some (police) who want to change, and who doesn't feel really good about this. I heard from one of my friends when they arrested him, that one of them told his colleagues to stay calm, and act normal. So there are persons who doesn't want to do it in this way, but they are pushed to do it. By their chiefs. By the power.

When the police came... I remember it was Saturday. And they told me that they just wanted to talk with me. "We want to... just have a conversation with you in the police station." I said ok, and got in the car. But when we went, I could see it was not the way to the police station, it was out of the city. I asked one police "what is happening?" He told me: "We changed our mind, now we will go to Åstorp detention center." And they put me in detention for 8 months.
(pause)
I still get nervous a little bit, when I am talking about Åstorp, because it was very... dark days. Many people maybe they don't know about this, especially Swedish people. They think it's like a hotel for foreign people. But it is a prison. A prison for people who have committed no crime.

Me, I don't fear them. After what I have gone through…
I don't fear anything. Are you police? No, no, no, I don't fear
you. Because you are a human being, like me. You cannot destroy me. If you beat me… ok, we're in Sweden, it's your
country, so maybe you can beat me here. But if you come
with me to Africa, I will also make sure that you won't come
back! Because of the treatment you have given me here,
in Malmö, in Sweden.

The texts above are excerpts from the script of the theater production The Malmö Code, An introduction to the paralell Society which had it's premiere in Malmö November 2014.

The script consists of texts from interviews and survey responses given by Border Police, Social Services, other citizens who interact with undocumented migrants through work or commitment, as well as interviews with people with present or former experience of living undocumented. All witnesses live and/or work in Malmö. The material was processed and put together to a script by the playwright and dramaturge Cecilia Nkolina. I was part of staging the production as a Director. Together with an ensamble of fourteen people, (one actress, one musician, one producer and eleven people with the experience of living undocumented) voice and body is given to these testemonies during a 100 minute long performance.

This is the second performance made by Theatre InterAkt together with and about the situation of undocumented migrants in Sweden.

Between 2010 and 2012 Theatre InterAkt was asked by the asylums and No Borders movement in Malmö to take part in a project of making a musical. The theme of the musical – the politics of migration and the situation of undocumented migrants in Europe and Sweden. The playwrites, actors and musicans of the musical, activists in the asylum- rights and No Borders movement, some living undocumented at the time. The result, a performance that was invited to play on the National Stage in Stockholm's National Theatre.

The fact that the musical aroused many
requsts from people interested to take part in
theatre projects on this topic, through tes-
temonies/interviews, writings and through
acting, led us to continue, to go deeper. In
the No Border Musical Project, the witnesses
came from those with the experiences of
living as undocumented and/or being an activist in the asylum-rights/No Border movement.
In The Malmö Code many more voices are
heard. At the same time the focus is very local.
And our local perspective continues when
we, during 2015, pass on more theatrical tools
as a motor for social change within a community theatre that was started by a group of
young undocumented and ex-undocumented
migrants together with Theatre InterAkt.
Three performances will take place in different
locations in Malmö from February to September 2015.

Due to confidentiality, we can only publish the
materials that we received approval for from
participants to share outside the theater's room.
We have no such approval from the Police
nor the Social Service; but from 3 people with
the experience of living undocumented
in Sweden have choosen to share their material (processed by the dramaturge) for
this publication.

presented by Sara Larsdotter
– Director – Theatre InterAkt

freedom of movement

BEING NOWHERE

TRAVELERS
RIGHTS
RAILWAY
PLATFORM

FREEDOM
MEANS
FREEDOM
TRADING

NO
BORDERS

TIAL EXPERIMENT

MIGRATION RIGHTS

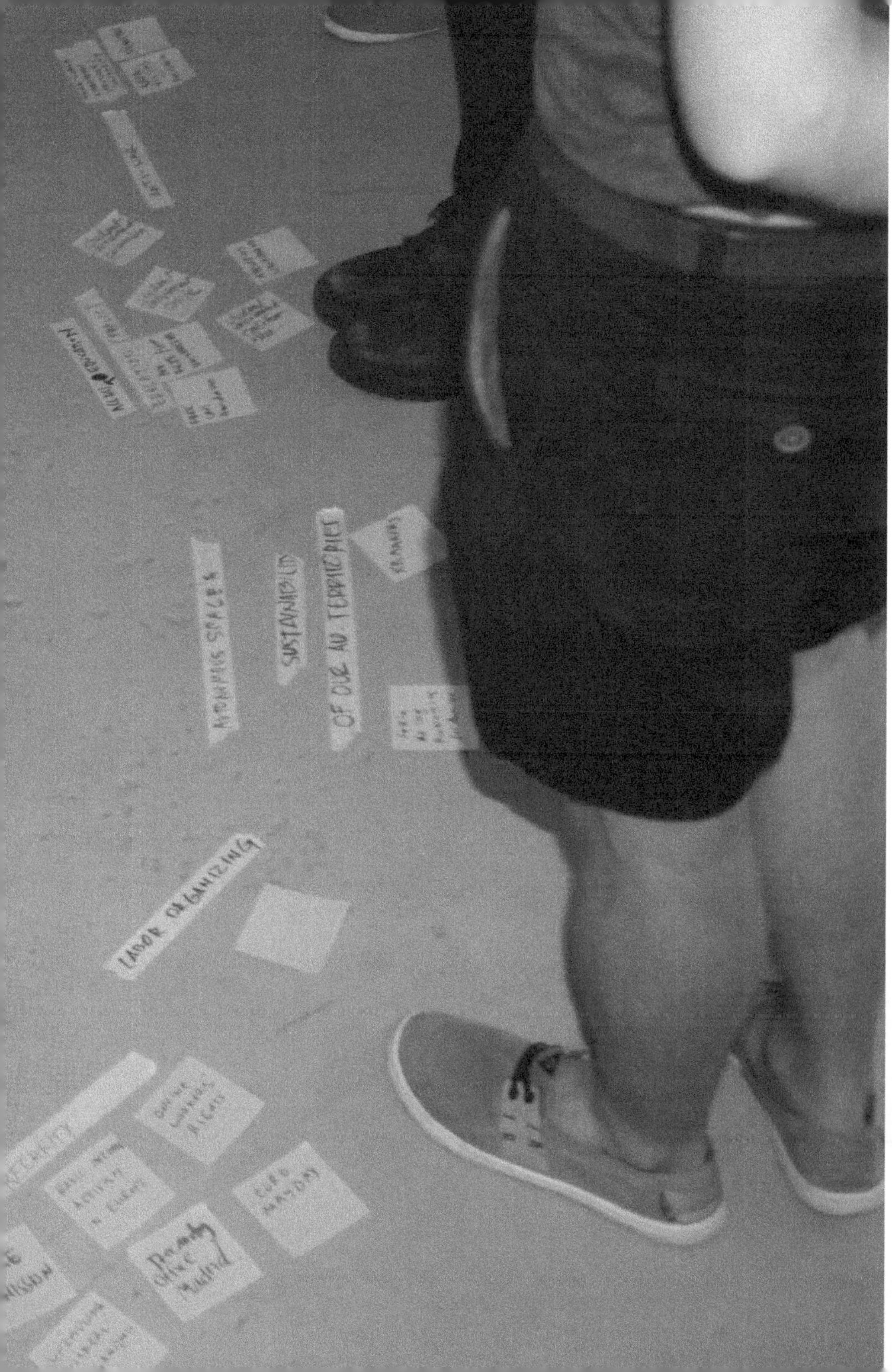
SUSTAINABILITY
LABOR ORGANIZING

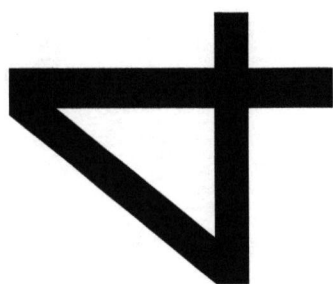

Tactics

f-r-a-g-m-e-n-t-o-s periféricos y reflexiones Atlánticas

by Claudia Delso

PERIPHERAL
FRAGMENTS AND
ATLANTIC
REFLECTIONS.

(1)

(desire)

... moving myself

(2)

from,

within and towards the
periphery

I situate myself along the border, in the road without asphalt,
in the forgotten stone house left alone in the brushwood.
Desire, necessity: they transform the manner of returning.
I needed to situate and displace myself at the same time.
I found orientation at this pause. At this initial point. A point of
departure known or (re-)cognized as that which will to
depart, again. Im at the point of departure.

(3)

Three words
surround the stone:

risk, crisis, invention[1]
displacement, orientation, situating[2]

(4)

I can see myself reflected in the pool.
It has stopped raining, but there's still no sun. Not yet.

1   Transit7, International Women's Theatre Festival and Meeting,
Holstebro, 2013.
2   Situating oneself, Embodied Practiques, Espai Electrodoméstica,
Barcelona, 2014.

(5)

Come with me?

   It's not that I want you to move, but I want you to come,
to come and see from the other side. From here you can see
far way, you can observe with perspective, I guess the
sea helps to observe the horizon and it's suspended points
in the void.
   Should we move?

(6)

   Look:

                              do you see?
   I can move the body, displace weight, change my gaze's
orientation. Instead of a known route, I decide to change
direction, assume the risk to stay, steady, stop myself. It's the
same place but with another appearance, an immediate
look, the gaze of the other (you). My own glaze that looks
different, gazes peripherally. (As Marina Garcés would say)

(7)

   The periphery:
                     It is done or undone?
   And if the center disappears, do we still have a periphery?
   And the periphery?
   Did we make ourselves peripheries?
                     Do we make peripheries?
   Who submits to   Can the center itself
   the center's center?   be displaced?

                     ATLANTIC
                     REFLECTIONS

   From the peripheries of Galicia, where to not emigrate
is synonymous with rebellion, to stay and cultivate the immediate setting is a quasi-revolutionary acts. As I listen to the
incessant rhythm of endless rain, I decide to stop looking to
what might be in front of me and look to what I have by my
side, this other empty and unnoticed periphery. To remove the

center from its role as protagonistic, to revindicate the whats in proximity, what is close.

From this profile, the necessity to stay, to be, and to share other forms of doing, living, and surviving from a peripheral place as Galicia (A Coruña to be more precise) is born. From this city a political artifact named Marea Altántica has emerged, it's a citizenship platform and process of participation, a possibility to both think and act politically the city where one lives. Recuperating the scale of what is possible. La Marea (The tide) was born as an hypothesis, as one of the processes of political confluence and municipalism unfolding in Spain in this last year (Guanyem Barcelona, Ganemos Madrid, etc). It's a project with a specific and concrete scenario: The municipal elections of 2015, but independent of what might happen, this hypothesis its becoming flesh in the city, and that supposes a displacement from the apathy and the inertia that has been installed on and with us. Personally, this whole process is making me re-situate myself in the city where I was born, to change my focus and allowed myself to displace certain grudges, up to the point of discovering that in this peripheral city in which everything seemed to arrive some years late, there's no need to migrate to feel part .

A few days ago, I went on a stroll with Xurxo Souto (singer, writer and multifaceted coruñés) along the outline of coast that borders our city. The stroll had a name: A typonomy of perceivable stones on de la Torre Peninsula, or an encounter with the big sea for a few meters with our city.

A walk through memory, a walk along the periphery of the periphery. At the end of the walk we shouted, Medre o mar! ¡Medre! (Grow the sea! Grow!)

An Inventory of Presence

by Jara Rocha

I take notes from time to time, while present in places I go,
in conversation with the friends and colleagues with whom
I think and read with. Together we try to make close readings
of the matters that seem to characterize the exceptional conditions of our times, or that have something to say about it.

"An inventory of presence" is an attempt to turn these
notes into a tool for permutation; a tool for conducting, breaking or bypassing a preset of coordinates. It is a jumper. A
location-sourced text. As a presentation of time and space, it
can be read. As a representation of situatedness, it might
be inhabited.

It is a body of parts, an embodied text of parts; perhaps.
Presented in part, it is an invitation to jump upon and
within presence. Whatever it means to be present, here.
Whenever is present. Now. Ready to permute. Mutate.
Made to permutate.

Southern Europe, May 2015.

tactics

	actants	gestures/manners	time	scales	conditions
A	ALGORITHM		ago	ABUNDANCE	ACTUAL
	ALPHABET	ADDRESS			AFFORDABILITY
	ARCHIVE	AFFECT		ACTUAL	AVAILABILITY
	AURA	APPROACH			CENTRIFUGAL
B	BACKGROUND	BORROW	at	AFFINITY	CENTRIPETAL
	BEING	BREED			COMMON
	BELIEF	CARE		COMMUNITY	CONTINUITY
	BLOOM	CONNECT			DENSE
	BODY PARTS	CONVERGE	before	CONTINGENCY	DIFFRACTION
	BORDER	DECLUTCH			DISTORTION
C	CODE	DELEGATE		DIALOGICAL	DISTRIBUTED
	COLLECTIVE	DIFFRACT	by		DURABILITY
D	DATA	DISOBEY		EDUCATIONAL	ENCRYPTION
	DISCOURSE	DISPOSSESS			EVENTUALITY
E	ESSENCE	DISAPPEAR	for	EPHEMERAL	FUTURE
F	FORM	DISSENT			GENERATIONAL
	FORMULA	DISSOLVE		FINITUDE	GROUP
G	GENDER	EMANCIPATE	in		HUMAN
	GENDER-CHANGER	EMERGE		FREEDOM DEGREES	INTELLIGIBILITY
	actants	gestures/manners	time	scales	conditions

space	crossings/ ambients	coord	named frames	conjunctions	methods
above	ABOUT PAGE	and	ACTOR-NET-WORK-THEORY	after	BOTTOM-UP
	AESTHETICS				CAETERIS PARIBUS
	AFFECTS			although	CARTOGRAPHY
	ANARCHISM		AUTOETHNOG-RAPHY		
across	ANTHROPO-CENE			as	CODEX
	ARCHITEC-TURE	but		as if	CONSTITUTION
	ARCHIVE			as long as	
	ART		CYBERNETICS	as though	
at	CLASS				CULTURAL MEDIATION
	COMMONS		DECOLONIAL	because	DEFINITION
	COMMUNITY	for			
	POSSIBILITY			before	DESCRIPTION
below	CONFLICT		DIALOG		
	CTHULHUCENE			even if	DISANTHOPO-CENTRIFY
	DEMOCRACY			even though	DISCOURSE ANALYSIS
	DOMESTIC	nor			DRAG
beside	EDITORIAL		EURACA	if	DRIVE (DERIVE)
	EFFICIENCY			if only	ENCRYPTION
	EROTICS				EXPEDITION
space	crossings/ ambients	coord	named frames	conjunctions	methods

tactics

	actants	gestures/manners	time	scales	conditions
H	HISTORY	ENUNCIATE			MALLEABILITY
	HUMAN			GEOLOGICAL	NAME
I	INFORMATION	FACE	later		NOMADISM
	INSTRUCTIONS	FAKE		INFRASTRUC-TURAL	OPACITY
	INTERFACE				ORALITY
	INTERFERENCE	FOCUS		INHUMAN	ORDERED
L	LOBBY	FUCK	on		PAST
N	NAME	GIVE		NANO	PLAUSIBLE
	NON-HUMAN				POSSBILITY
O	OBJECT	LAY	past	NETWORK	POWER
	PERSONA	MEASURE			PRECARITY
P	PRIZE			SCARCITY	PREFERABILI-TY
R	README	MEDIATE			PRESENT
	RULE/ LAW	MOVE	since	STRATEGICAL	PRIORITY
S	SIGN				PROPERTY
	SITUATION	NAME		TACTICAL	PUBLIC
	SOCIAL CLASS	OCCUPY			QUALIFIED
	SOMA	ORDER	till	TRANSCEND-ENCE	QUANTIFIED
	actants	gestures/manners	time	scales	conditions

201

space	crossings/ambients	coord	named frames	conjunctions	methods
	ETHICS		HERMENEUTICS	in order that	FICTION
by	EXTITUTION	or		now that	
	FAITH		NEW CONCEPTUALISMS		GENERATIVE
	FREE UNIVERSITIES				GONZO
from	GENDER			once	HORIZONTAL
	GENERATION		NEW MATERIALISMS		INTERPRETATION
	GOVERNANCE	so		rather than	LIST
	IMPASSE				MANIFESTO
in	INFRASTRUCTURE			since	MODEL
	INSTITUTIONAL		NON-REPRESENTATIONAL		OBJECTOLOGY
	LOCAL			so that	OPACITY
	MARKET	yet			PARAMETRIC
into	NAMES		OBJECT ORIENTED ONTOLOGY		PARTICIPANT
	NEOLIBERALISM			than	PATTERNS
	NEW MUNICIPALISMS				RADICAL PROMISCUITY
	PARLIAMENT		PIIGS	that	RADICAL SYMMETRY
next to	POLITICS		POST-SNOWDEN		
	PUBLIC SPACE			though	RELATOGRAMA

space | crossings/ambients | coord | named frames | conjunctions | methods

	actants	gestures/ manners	time	scales	conditions
S	SOURCE				REACHABILITY
	SUBJECT	ORIENT		VIRTUAL	RELATIONALI-TY
	SUPER-EGO		to		RESILIENCE
		PROTECT		ZONE	RIGIDNESS
U	UNAPPROPRI-ATED	PULL			SCRIPTABILITY
	UNAPPROPRIA-BLE	PUSH			SOVEREIGNITY
		REACT			TRANSPAREN-CY
	UNITY	REBEL	while		UTOPIC
V	VARIABLE	ROLL			VIRTUAL
	VOICE	SERVE			VOLUME
		SHARE			
W	WORD	TAKE			
		TAXONOMIZE			
		TRICK			
		TURN			
	actants	gestures/ manners	time	scales	conditions

space	crossings/ambients	coord	named frames	conjunctions	methods
	RESOURCES				
	SOCIAL MOVEMENTS		POSTHUMAN-ISM	till	RENDER
on	SOFT CAPITALISM				
	STANDARD			unless	REVERSE ENGINEERING
	SYMBOLIC CAPITAL			until	
	TENSION		QUEER / LGTBQI		TOP-DOWN
onto	TERRITORIAL			when	TOPOLOGY
	TERRORISM			whenever	TRANSDUC-TION
	THE SOCIAL		SITUATED KNOWLEDGE		
over	URBAN			where	
through				whereas	TRANSLATION
to			SPECULATIVE REALISM		
to-wards				wherever	
under			STANDPOINT	while	UNBLACKBOX-ING

space	crossings/ambients	coord	named frames	conjunctions	methods

Humor and Displacement

by Marc Herbst

Between giving a fuck and not exists a variety of difficult emotions; the pain of loss, grief, longing and failure are inherent in displacement. To not be able to, to not have received, to not have done what one thought one would do – these and other failures necessarily involve displacement. The object of desire which situated one thusly has not been realized; instead of happiness what is realized are the arrays of more difficult emotions.

To not give a fuck, to role one's eyes "whatever" doesn't necessarily mean "I don't care." Rather, "whatever" can be an instrument of survival, of just not letting the bastards get ya down.

"Whatever" doesn't necessarily mean to forget about whatever was hoped or the specific formation of the failure or loss. Queer critical theorists Judith Halberstam and queer artist collective LTTR said in the naughts, "practice more failure." This, in order that

collective life may be experienced more richly and so that the political efforts might reach towards victories in places where the limits of that context ultimately reveal themselves as bullshit in time, or actually more flexible then you might imagine.

But practicing more failure as a collective manifesto suggests a solidarity which has advanced a step beyond the particulars of this essay. Solidarity suggests, obviously, a collective practice between individuals. Rather, I'd rather focus on one particular role of humor as a form of intrapersonal solidarity; between myself and myself. Humor within displacement, besides memory may function as something more than Lauren Berlant's cruel optimism and something much less then Nietzsche's will. One could be ones own best friend.

Agamben's notion of "whatever" as explicated in The Coming Community is very particular. For him, "whatever" is an

205

ambiguous and insignificant thing, but only because whatever is whatever because it has actual connection to more stable universals. One says "whatever" because one knows something else is available – we say, "I wish I could have the red skittles, but whatever, I'll take the blue." We say, "I wished for full socialism and trumpets, but whatever, I'm punished with some form of market democracy and a trumpet." The strand remains, unfulfilled. But what also remains, if the loss is mediated in such a way that one can look at the wound, is a contextual example to learn from, a particular failure. One way to mediate the loss, is humor's interventions.

Solidarity appears again. As any student of subculture knows, affects produced around painful experience produce solidarity for those who find themselves in pain. While the king sits in the throne pleasuring himself on the fresh blood of the vanquished, the victims are technologizing their loss. Humor produces subtle discourses first in the

individual and then in the collective by which pain becomes something different. First a laugh, or (ok, its not humorous but) a song or maybe a fashion sense, or a way of walking. And then some new formation...

Gallows humor is not about looking forward to being hung. Dark humor is not necessarily committed to turning off the lights. Whatever is a comment to resolve the psychic tension within the person who utters it, but is rarely a word of surrender.

Life is cruel, but so is your mom. Sometime you have to run, like your butt. When things are terrible, you realize your just looking in the mirror. Anyplace is better then here, because your not drunk.

Everyone is a stranger... but then again,

do you really even know yourself?
You don't know
where your next meal
is going to come from, Hey!
Time for a diet.
You forgot how to "please",
good thing you've got a shiny knife.

Your friends are all gone,
Lets get this party started!
Scared of the cops,
but cops spelled backwards is spoc!
Lost again, note to self:
bring whiskey next time.
Dirty clothes and smelly shoes – how cute
– a princess in rags.

Unemployed – hell yeah!
Broke – and livin' high on the hog.
Depressed – black is the new black!

Lonely, go stand in a fucking crowd.

Self help books my ass.

Gospel of wealth, bullshit.
Fucking privatization, fucking thieves.
Fucking fuck shit fuck fuck.
I want revolution.

Bullshit job – jullshlit blob.
Border Control, Corder bontrol – mon dieu!
Midnight flight on a low cost line,
lidnight blight on a blow toast mine.

These bones will die and so will you.

laughter that greeks have fallen into after the crazy failure of everything in june (friends told me the summer has been one of absurdity and exhilaration, jokes circulating everywhere). Etc – sure that when you experience trauma, when your world is shattered, humour is key. And part of that humour can be saying 'whatever', to avoid falling into depression/guilt etc (though 'whatever' can also be depression). Now that goes for certain experiences/conditions, but I don't think it can just be generalised. When the middle class public at some talkshows or comedy acts laughs its head off about whatever, when all becomes relative for feel-good effects, that's different. That's a liberal cultivation of 'whatever' in the context of priviledge, which is steeped in consumerism, cultural relativism, also colonialism... the 'whatever' of those who can afford not to bother, of 'I crashed my car into the bridge... I don't care – i love it...' and also of western disorientation and non-situatedness.

The kind of attitude that all is the same, all is interchangeable and exchangeable. This is 'whatever' in the present, deeply problematic, being marketed to us all over (the counterweight to self-control and performance). It reflects a lack of criteria, of orientation, a total liberal subjectification. That temporal and contextual difference seems crucial to me. In that sense, I don't know where/how your text situates itself.

Score for Movement

by Cristina Ribas

Describe or diagram the short route
your body knows by memory.
Describe or diagram the short route
your body knows by memory,
and that you miss.
Describe or diagram the short route.
A very short one.

Use symbols that
recollect that movement.
Use symbols that
perform that movement.
Use symbols,
words, perspectives,
perceptions...

Let yourself be aware
of the reasons, ways, visions,
changes of state, encounters,
findings, locations, loss.
Let yourself be aware
of possible changes of state.
Let yourself be aware.

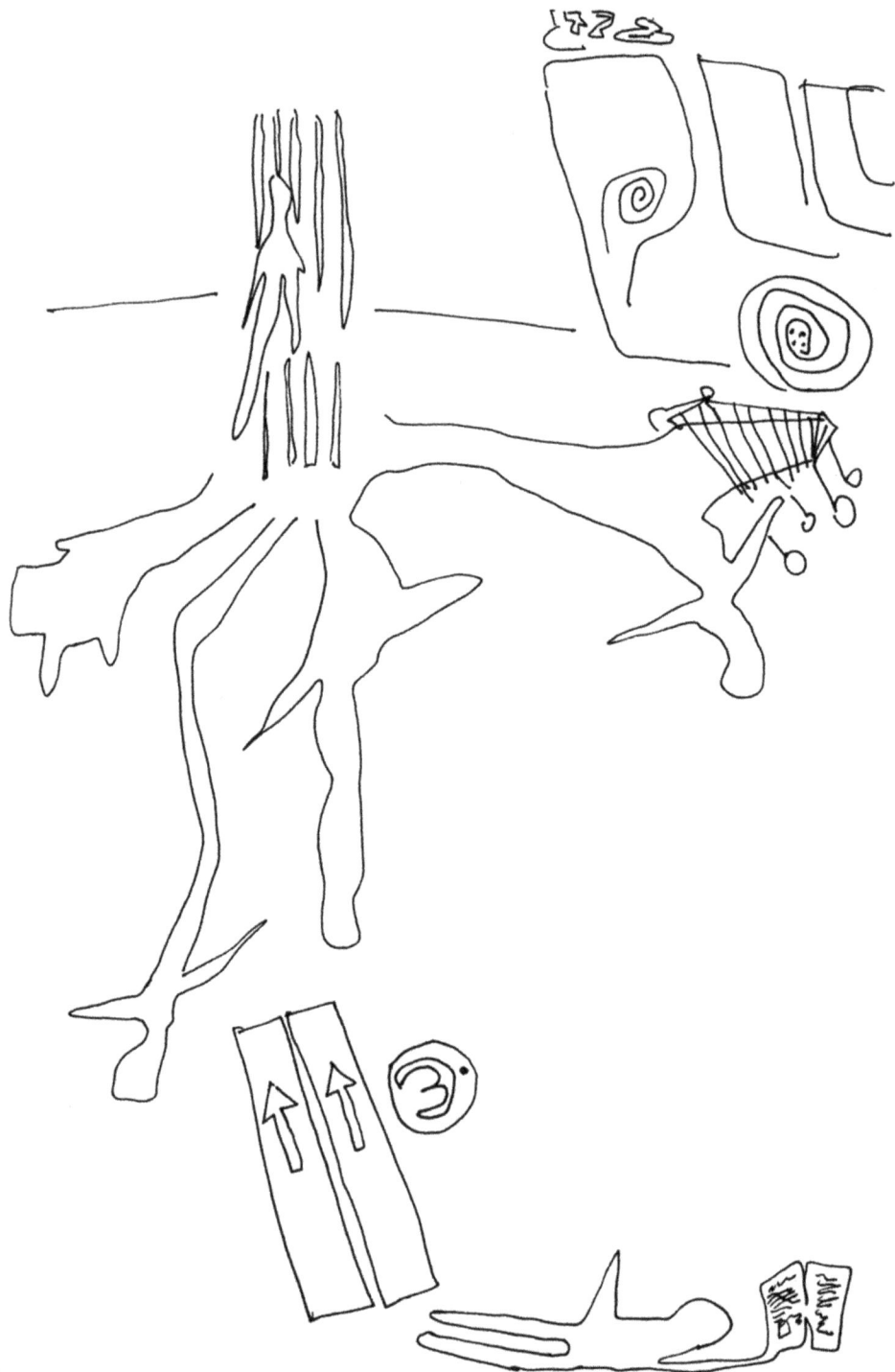

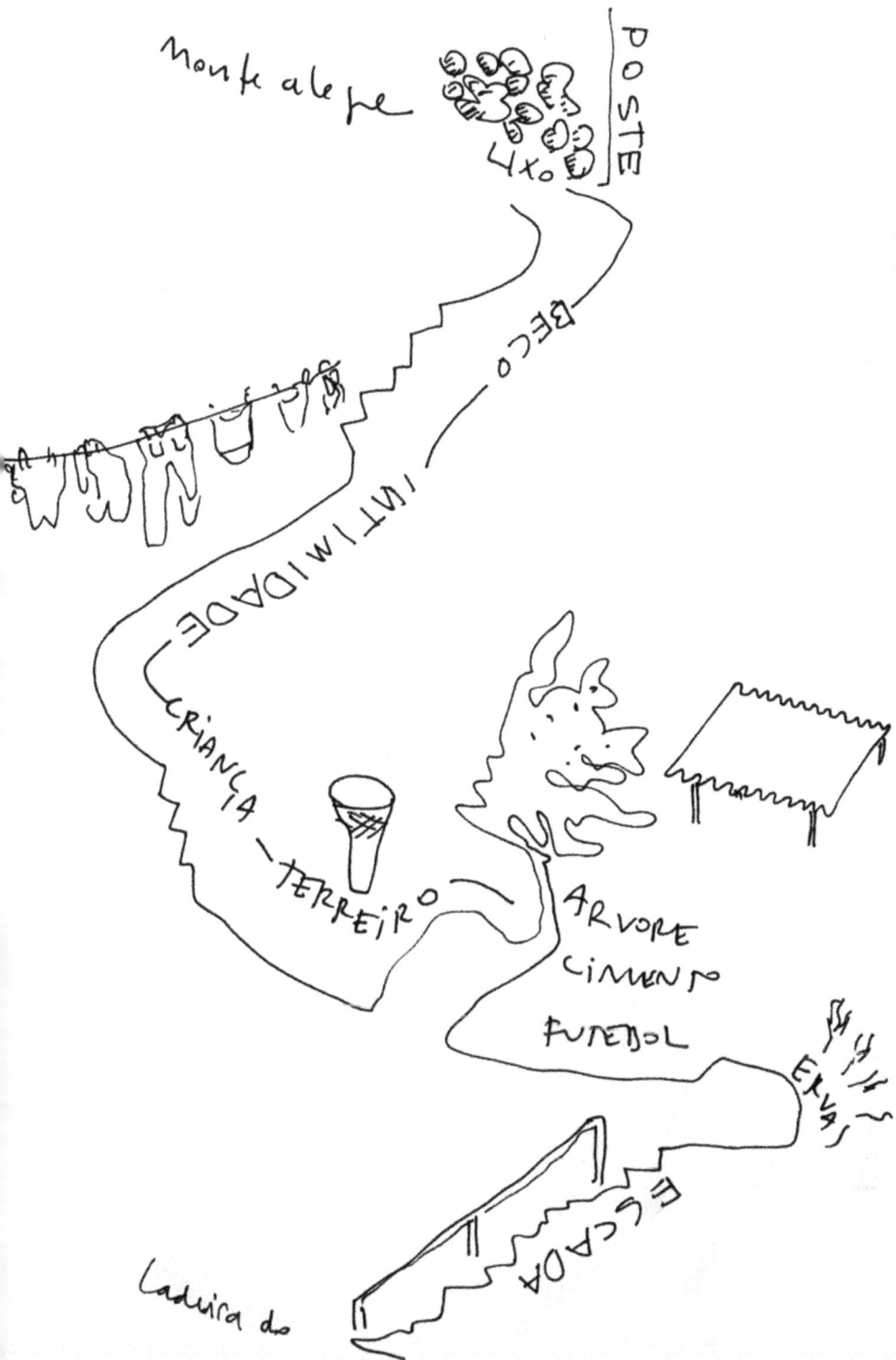

Monte alegre

POSTE

LIXO

BECO

INTIMIDADE

CRIANÇA

TERREIRO

ARVORE

CIMENTO

FUTEBOL

ERVAS

ESCADA

Ladeira do

213

Protocolo para movimento

by Cristina Ribas

Descreva ou diagrame um percurso pequeno
que você sabe de cor pela memória do seu corpo.
Descreva ou diagrame um percurso pequeno
que você sabe de cor pela memória do seu corpo
e do qual você sente saudade.
Descreva ou diagrame um percurso pequeno.
Um percurso muito pequeno.

Use símbolos que restituem aquele movimento.
Use símbolos que performem aquele movimento.
Use símbolos, palavras, perspectivas, percepções...

Deixe-se estar atento
às razões, modos, visões
mudanças de estado, encontros,
descobertas, localizações, perdas.
Deixe-se estar atento
a possíveis mudanças de estado.
Deixe-se estar atento.

Appendix

Alan Moore

I am about 3,580 miles from a place I love, ABC No Rio in lower Manhattan. I hope to be absolutely present at this moment which is always all I have.

Amit Rai

I'm ten steps away from my mother, sleeping, I am weeks away from feeling better.

Arnoldas

"I am 660 km away from Helsinki; in 1999, the first attempt at living somewhere else started there" – Ninaha

Bue Rübner Hansen

Bue lives 12,000 km away from the countries he has previously lived in, and sixteen generations away from a baker forefather who served on the city council of Mühlhausen after the city notables had overseen the brutal slaughter of the rebellious peasants who had taken over the city under the leadership of Thomas Müntzer under the slogan: Omnia Sunt Communia.

Claire English

An app on my phone tells me it is eleven days since I ovulated. I am twenty four hour flight followed by a twenty four minute drive from a pro-choice rally in Brisbane where all of my militant friends from my youth are waving banners and shouting out loud.

Claudia Delso es facilitadora cultural y consellera de participación en la ciudad de A Coruña.

Cristina Ribas lives 10,459.05 km far from latin american gaucho pampa where she was born and is 35 years away from the amnesty movement that ended dictatorship in Brazil.

Grupo Esquizo
We live around 984 feeds from la Electrodoméstica space where we share our lives and we are 5,4 years away from the first Skizo meeting where we read collectively firstly.

Jara Rocha
1984: Sarajevo's winter Olympics, the commercialization of iconographic computerism and Michel Foucault's death from complications derived from AIDS, coinciding with the moment when a peruvian male and a catalan female

facilitated the emergence of a cluster of so-called human cells, which they officially registered under the civil name of "Jara". This cluster started its socialization and cultural formatting in the immediate surroundings of 40° 43′ 37″ N, 3° 10′ 37″, geopolitically also known – depending on scale and tone – as Castilla, Iberic Peninsula or the PIIGS territories. In 2015, it inhabits the tension of two sovereignity-affected spots, aeronautically known as BCN & BXL.

Julius is a decade away from reading – with great curiosity – a phrase written by a traveller: to have no more a place to return [home]. He is also a long and diverse trajectory away from (peace with) his own body.

Laura Lapinskiene
At the moment, I am some 689 weeks away from the day I met my fellow traveler, which changed the course of my journey, and 11,000 km from Yogyakarta, Indonesia, where I left part of my soul.

Manuela Zechner is 1,300 km south-west from the alpine mountain place that feels like her (impossible) home, four years from the UK student movement which felt like a real awakening, and still (possibly interminably) processing her recent displacements across the uncanny European continent.

Marc Herbst
I am in a small room thinking about the room next door. I will be leaving the house soon.

Nizaiá Cassián (script), Raquel Sánchez, Miriam Sol, Lucía Serra (dynamization). We have been walking together since 2010, trying to sediment modes of encounter, spaces of oral and conversational weaving of thought and affective experimentation. We come from Grupo Esquizo Barcelona traversed by the interest of producing collective, contingent and situated thinking around micropolitics and the schizoanalytic practice, looking for the invention of collective care assemblages, purring around the composition of liveable lives in the contemporary city.

Paula Cobo-Guevara is at no distance from a mediterranean city which con-

stantly teaches her new affects and knowings – after a long drift, a territory which enables her different modes of transference and healing to a long and narrow country facing the south pacific ocean and it's disappeared bodies.

Sara Larsdotter
I am approximately 2600 nautical miles away from a good starting point for crossing the atlantic ocean sailing. I am one year and four months away from the death of my grandmother.

These biographies are inspired by Chto Delat's video-performance "The excluded. In a moment of danger." http://vimeo.com/channels/chtodelat/109670074#t=162s

CREDITS

p. 22 Claudia del Fierro
p. 23 (below)
       Lucia Engaña

COLOPHON

Situating ourselves in displacement: conditions, experiences and subjectivity across neoliberalism and precarity.

Edited by Manuela Zechner, Paula Cobo-Guevara and Marc Herbst.

Released by Journal of Aesthetics & Protest Press, Leipzig and Minor Compositions, Colchester, 2017. Distributed by Autonomedia. Designed by Anja Kaiser. Typeface by Filip Matejicek.

Minor Compositions is a series of interventions and provocations drawing from autonomous politics, avant-garde aesthetics, and the revolutions of everyday life. Minor Compositions is an imprint of Autonomedia www.autonomedia.org

223

224

conditions

This book emerges out of the "Situating Ourselves inDisplacement" autumn laboratory that took place in Barcelona in autumn 2014, organised by Manuela Zechner and Paula Cobo-Guevara and contributed to by a series of facilitators and participants, all of whom we would like to thank here. Your co-funding of this publication has made it possible to go to print finally! Thanks also to Anja Kaiser for her generous design work.